Dedication

This book is dedicated in particular to the brothers of Enlightenment Lodge #198 and East Denver Lodge #160- who have helped me find wisdom, strength and beauty as I have traveled in Freemasonry. This work could also not be possible without the previous research done on the subject by brothers Albert Pike, Gerard Encause, Kevin Townley, Kirk McKnulty, Manly P. Hall, and the works of Aryeh Kaplan. Each of their works are in many ways far superior to this, but I offer this book as a new perspective from where they have left off. It is also dedicated to all those seeking further light on their quest, and to the Unknown Superiors who help to guide them. Finally, I dedicate this book to my wife Rosa- as this work would not be possible without her patience and support.

Table of Contents

The 32 Secret Paths of Solomon
A New Examination of the Qabbalah in Freemasonry

Introduction:

Qabbalah is a rich tradition of symbolic study dealing with the emanation of aspects of Deity within the framework of symbolism, letter and number. This tradition has been carefully preserved and perpetuated over the years through various Hebrew qabbalistic schools and to a certain degree within the mystery school traditions of the western world. In fact, the very word "qabbalah" means "tradition"- or "to receive", and therefore we are being entrusted with receiving this tradition. Many of the ideas of qabbalah have been passed down from teacher to student, relatively un-altered, over several centuries. There have been fundamental qabbaltistic texts like the *Sephir Yetzirah*, the *Zohar*, and the *Sephir Bahir*, which have provided the backbone of study in this symbolic art. There have also been lesser known qabbalistic texts which deal with alchemy and the property of numbers and emanations like the *Aesch Mezareph* and the *Sephir Sephiroth*. Different qabbalistic scholars debate on what the most important qabbalistic work is, with most suggesting it is the *Zohar*- a text compiled in the thirteenth century and written in Aramaic. It consists largely of commentaries on the Pentateuch- the first five books of the Old Testament. Others consider the *Sephir Yetzirah* as the most important qabbalistic text, as it offers a main list of symbolic correspondences, and some have deemed it the oldest qabbalistic text- going back to the origins of the Hebrew tradition. I will primarily draw from these two texts in this book, as both illustrate well the idea that secret elements exist in Hebrew and Greek scripture, (along with Masonic ritual). The qabbalistic doctrine is based on the idea that the universe is a manifestation of God's thought; thought is expressed by speech; speech is composed of letters; and thereby letters can be the symbolic link that reveals the hidden nature of all things, and by extension, God's thoughts.

The qabbalistic system has also been translated from Hebrew into English with various authors arguing on whether the word "qabbalah" should begin with a "q", a "k", or a "c". I am not so concerned with which letter in English should be the beginning of this word, and I have chosen to use a "q"- only because this is what many of my teachers on the subject have used. Symbolically, "Q" in Hebrew is "Qoph", and it was associated with the back of the head- and particularly the extension of the nape of the neck, which was deemed an important center of activity in mystical pursuits. The word "Qabal" in Hebrew, meaning "to receive", begins with "qof"- equivalent to the English "Q". Therefore "Q" in the word "qabbalah" is as good as any for our use. Still others have used "K" or "C" because they relate to the Hebrew letter "Kaf", which has been associated with the image of a bent hand receiving something.

I would also like to emphasize that I am not of a traditional Jewish background, and I did not learn qabbalah within any particular Jewish qabbalistic school- though I have studied it with many different Rabbis, from various traditions over the years, who have been kind enough to indulge my genuine interests in the subject. These Rabbis belonged to one or another of various schools of initiation that I have belonged to. My primary study of the subject comes from my initiations into various western esoteric schools, and as such, this book may be providing an interpretation which has culminated from years of study within the systems of Freemasonry, Martinism, Rosicrucianism, Templarism, and various alchemical currents and Orders. As such, the book may provide a different perspective on the subject than most that are currently in publication. I should also mention that I began the study of qabbalah after having spent several years studying alchemy. The spiritual science of alchemy relies heavily on qabbalistic interpretation of the Bible and alchemical texts, and it is my belief that the degrees of Freemasonry outline alchemical operations, which also tie to qabbalah- as mentioned in *The Alchemical Keys to Masonic Ritual*. In my studies, I began to notice what I can only suggest appear to be inconsistencies within traditional qabbaltistic teachings- particularly related to the "Qabbalistic Tree". These are symbol systems that appear to me to be relatively forced interpretations in order to make a contrived pattern work. There is one cardinal esoteric rule that I learned very early on in alchemy, and this is that the old Masters of the Art would always put blinds in their publications that were revealed to the world. These blinds were put in so that the true initiates would learn the correct order to the work via a mouth to ear process. Owing to the fact that most of the early European qabbalistic texts received publication via the European alchemists, it seemed to me that there is a good possibility that blinds were added to the early qabbalistic diagrams and texts- which have been passed down as gospel to the current day within Western schools.

With this idea in mind, and based on an attempt to link the qabbalistic method with the alchemical work I was doing in the lab, a new pattern began to emerge, which I personally feel is a more correct and accurate interpretation of the qabbalistic texts and qabbalistic tree diagram, and of which seems to match and reflect perfectly with the rituals found within Freemasonry. As such, a warning should be given to the reader that much of what is being published in this book has not been found in publication previously, and I do so knowing full well that it is bound to upset a number of people who have come to interpret qabbalah in one or another particular light. To me, qabbalah is like a mirror, and it can reflect what you wish to see- and therefore can be subject to different interpretations. However, there have been dogmatic systems that have developed within several esoteric schools on how to interpret qabbalah over the years. There have been several schools created specifically to teach one interpretation of the symbolism. I am not attempting to de-value what these schools have to teach, nor am I trying to diminish their interpretation. I am just hoping to show that there is another way of looking at it, and if it is viewed within this new light, then it begins to explain in an easy and clear manner several previously ambiguous teachings. It also begins to bring new light to the degrees of Freemasonry and the mystery tradition it has perpetuated. This examination will also prove of value to those who are Martinists, as the initiations of Freemasonry and Martinism share much in common in the essential symbolic details- which is only natural since the Martinist system largely came out of Freemasonry, and Martinists later had a large influence on the composition of many of the "higher degrees" in Freemasonry.

I should also mention that I had no desire to ever write a book on so arcane and complex a system as qabbalah, and with as many books as there are on the subject out there, I thought the world may be best off just studying what has already been written. However the revelations I experienced in relation to my own qabbalistic studies and the relation of these studies to my personal alchemical work were just too incredible to be ignored. After having shared these revelations with several friends who are qabbalistic scholars within the field, they encouraged me whole-heartedly to get this information in publication, as they saw it as too valuable to ever become lost again…if indeed it was so. Within Freemasonry itself, in the fourth degree of the Ancient and Accepted Scottish Rite (SJ), we are likewise taught that qabbalah is the key to Freemasonry, and in fact, Freemasonry cannot be understood unless one has at least a preliminary understanding of qabbalah. Yet, how many brothers actually understand qabbalah or have even attempted to study it beyond what they are exposed to in the degrees or in general work like Pike's *Morals and Dogma*? Very few, and this is largely due to a relative intimidation of beginning study of such a complex and arcane subject matter. Therefore, as a result of the nudges of academic friends and brothers, and a general feeling that Masonic education needs to be further advanced, I have put this book together. My hope is that it will allow the student of qabbalah and the student of Freemasonry, to see a new pattern which will provide further light. I also hope this book to be a bridge that will help introduce the subject to new students so that they can better appreciate what some of the more complex writings on the subject have to offer.

I will therefore endeavor in this book to provide some general background of traditional interpretations, together with the new revelations on the subject, so that both the old and the new student of qabbalah can gain multiple perspectives. Ultimately, I hope that these ideas will work to be empowering to those who read it on a very personal level, and will help to bring each reader closer to the Grand Architect of the Universe. I should also mention that those initiated within Freemasonry will undoubtedly gain more out of this book then those who have not. However traditional qabbalistic scholars who are not Freemasons should also find value from these interpretations. For those studying this book who are not Freemasons, it is enough that you understand that the rituals of Freemasonry rest heavily on the story associated with the building of King Solomon's Temple- which features heavily in qabbalistic tradition. Those who are Freemasons may find that their tradition does indeed hide great secrets.

Chapter 1: What is Qabbalah?

What is Qabbalah? There are as many answers to this question as there are people who study qabbalah, and thousands of books on the subject out there in publication to prove it, but I will attempt a general answer. Qabbalah is a system of symbolic study designed to impart light on the manifestations of God in creation. If God created all things, and God is in all things, through his words, then He can manifest different aspects of Himself via the forms of creation itself. Therefore in studying creation, we can come to a better understanding of God. Letter forms, which are a product of human consciousness and by extension the consciousness of God, can also have a symbolic value associated with them, and as such, the written word can take on several layers of meaning, and can be an expression of the force behind the words of creation itself. Qabbalah then is an attempt to understand these symbolic patterns and be able to read the deeper aspects of both sacred texts and nature, and see how both are manifestations of a greater consciousness that we are fundamentally connected with. The chief religious text for both Jewish and Christian qabbaltists has been the Bible. However other texts were written to further explore these ideas and to act as meditation vehicles. These texts, like the *Sephir Yetzirah*, the *Zohar*, the *Sephir Bahir*, the *Aesch Mezareph,* and others, have many passages in them that describe a particular symbolic diagram that represents the expression of consciousness in creation, and this has been called the "Qabbalistic tree"- or sometimes the "Tree of Life", the "Tree of knowledge", "Jacob's

Ladder" or the "Qabbalistic Pillars", among other things. For our purposes, we will just call it "the Qabbalistic Tree". Though different qabbalistic schools represent the Tree somewhat differently, there are certain fundamental aspects to it which are universal. It should also be mentioned that even though qabbalah embodies more than just the qabbalistic tree, the qabblaistic tree embodies much of qabbalistic teachings. It is the storage container for the various qabbalistic teachings.

In general, this Tree is composed of 10 spheres- called sephiroth, (with sometimes a hidden 11th sphere), along with 22 paths that connect these spheres- each of which is represented by one of the 22 Hebrew letters, and they rest on three pillars. Thus there are a total of 32 emanations of Deity, with a possible 33rd hidden emanation. The set up of these three pillars and the 22 paths is found in the *Sephir Yetzirah*, where it says that God "created a reality out of nothing, called nonentity into existence and hewed, as it were, colossal pillars from intangible air... He predetermined, and by speaking created every creature and every word by one name. For an illustration may serve the twenty two elementary substances by the primitive substance of Aleph." These three pillars have been represented by the two pillars on the outer porch of King Solomon's Temple and the third pillar of man standing between them. The outside pillars represented the pair of opposites that can only be reconciled by the middle pillar standing between them. In this light, it may be interpreted that King Solomon's pillars are a model of the pillars created by God. In Freemasonry, these three pillars are likewise represented by the senior officers of every Lodge- the Master, Senior Warden, and Junior Warden (who every Master Mason at one point assumes the role of). The ten spheres with the 22 paths are likewise described in the Qabbalistic text of the Zohar (V, 85): "These twenty-two letters which are inscribed in the Torah are illustrated in the Ten Creative utterances. Each of those ten, which are crowns of the King, is traced in certain letters. Hence the

Holy Name is disguised under other letters and each utterance leads to one above it certain letters, so that they are comprised in one another. Therefore we trace the Holy Name in other letters not its own, one set being concealed in the other, though they are linked together. He who desires to know the combinations of the holy names must know the letters which are inscribed in each crown and then combine them."

Also in the Zohar, (III, 278) we read: "For the Torah is the name of the Holy One, blessed be He. As the name of the Holy One is engraved in Ten Words (creative utterances) of Creation, so is the whole Torah engraved in the Ten Words, and these Ten Words are the name of the Holy One, and the whole Torah is thus one Name, the Holy Name of God Himself. Blessed is he who is worthy of her, the Torah, for he will be worthy of the Holy Name."

Entire books have gone into detail writing about this Qabbalistic Tree, along with what Hebrew letters correlate with which paths, and which planets correlate with which sephiroth. We will explore some of these theories as we go along. In general, this Tree represents a blue print for creation on all levels, and it becomes a mandala that we can meditate on in order to make correlations in the book of nature and within ourselves. Each sphere or path represents an aspect of the manifestation of the consciousness of Deity in creation. On the next page are three different versions of the Qabbalistic Tree which have been developed over the centuries. The "natural array" version is according to a system called "the Gra", the second version is one used by some older schools of qabbalah, and the last one is a version used by the Safed School, which is based on the *Zohar*. For our purposes, we will be using the version used by the Safed School, as in my mind it takes into consideration more aspects of the qabbalistic science than the others, and I will show how it correlates perfectly with what the qabbalistic text of the *Sephir Yetzirah* has to say.

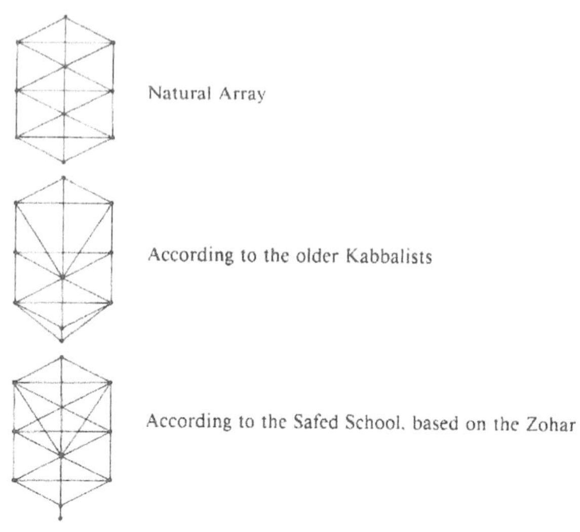

The Qabbalistic tradition also found symbolic associations with the actual 22 Hebrew letters themselves. Each letter was not only divided in special categories (mother, double and simple), but each letter had other symbolic values to it. To begin with, each letter was named after a particular physical thing in the world that represented the letter's nature; so for example the Hebrew letter "Beth", equivalent to the English "B", meant "house" and was associated with a house. However there are further symbolic associations. The three "mother letters"- Aleph, Mem, and Shin (A, M, Sh)- corresponded with the elements of air, water, and fire respectively. The seven double letters (called double because they had both a hard and a soft pronunciation), corresponded to the seven planets and by extension both the positive and negative aspects associated with these planets in antiquity, and the alchemists recognized them as being associated with the seven noble metals and the seven liberal arts and sciences. The twelve single or simple letters corresponded to the twelve signs of the zodiac, and by extension, the 12 tribes of Israel. On top of these symbolic associations, qabbalistic texts like the *Sephir Yetzirah* further associated each letter with various parts of the human anatomy, days of the week, months of the year, and other symbolic associations. Likewise, each Hebrew letter was represented by a number- so the letters added up in a word could reveal a symbolic number pattern or association. The idea behind these symbolic associations is that the Hebrew alphabet represents a code, and if the code is known, then sacred text can be read in a new light. Below is attached a diagram which shows some of these correlations. Some esoteric traditions have likewise made notice of the fact that within human DNA there are 23 sets of chromosomes, but the 23rd is what determines sex. Therefore every person alive, whether man or woman, share the trait of 22 chromosomes, and if we go with the idea of a soul being androgynous, it would be composed of 22 "spiritual chromosomes"- which falls in line very nicely with the 22 Hebrew letters which are said to make up the human constitution. There are some qabbalistic schools which suggest that there is a hidden 23rd letter of the Hebrew alphabet, but this is beyond the scope of this book.

Hebrew	Name	English	Number	Derivation	Association	Symbol
א	Aleph	A	1	Ox	Air	🜁
ב	Beth	B	2	House	Moon	☽
ג	Gimel	G	3	Camel	Mars	♂
ד	Dalet	D	4	Door	Sun	☉
ה	He	H/E	5	Window	Aries	♈
ו	Vau	V,Fv	6	Hook or nail	Taurus	♉
ז	Zayin	Z	7	Weapon	Gemini	♊
ח	Cheth	Ch	8	Fence or hedge	Cancer	♋
ט	Teth	T	9	Cross in circle	Leo	♌
י	Yod	I,Y	10	Hand	Virgo	♍
כ, ך	Kaph	K,C	20/500	Hallow of hand	Venus	♀
ל	Lamed	L	30	Goad	Libra	♎
מ, ם	Mem	M	40/600	Water	Water	🜄
נ, ן	Nun	N	50/700	Fish	Scorpio	♏
ס	Samech	S	60	Prop or support	Sagitarius	♐
ע	Ayin	O	70	Eye or well	Capricorn	♑
פ, ף	Phe	P	80/800	Mouth	Mercury	☿
צ, ץ	Tzadi	Tz	90/900	Fisher	Aquarius	♒
ק	Qof	Q	100	Back of head	Pisces	♓
ר	Resh	R	200	Head	Saturn	♄
ש	Shin	Sh	300	Tooth	Fire	🜂
ת	Tav	Th	400	Sign of cross	Jupiter	♃

Above: Associations according to the *Sephir Yetzitrah.*

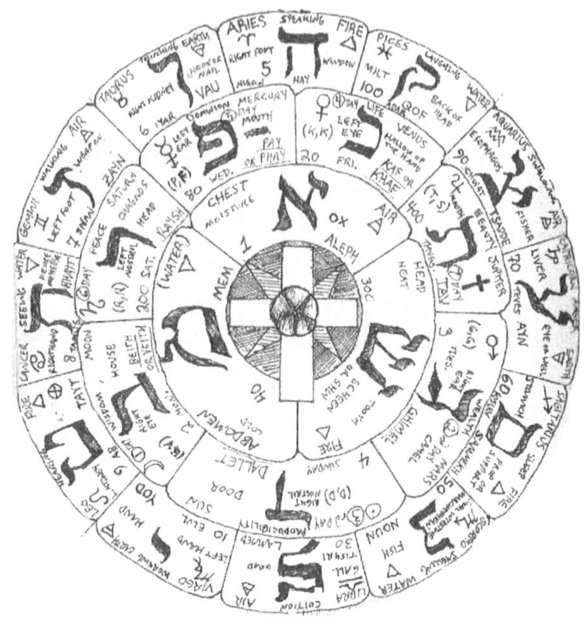

Above: The qabbalistic rose cross with the petals of the rose representing each Hebrew letter and their associations.

Ultimately these correlations were all meant to be guid posts, or symbolic representations of the different ways energy, and by extension consciousness, can manifest in the world. By understanding how energy interacts we can use it and work with it to bring about constructive manifestations in the world. Seemingly antagonistic oppositions can be reconciled in harmony, and ultimately through our consciousness breakthrough and development we in turn glorify God through his creation.

There has been much debate on the antiquity of qabbalistic systems, with some scholars arguing that the system goes all the way back into ancient Egypt, and that it was inherited by the Hebrews there, and other scholars suggesting that it was a manifestation of the middle ages. I am not going to explore this history or argument in this book, though I am of the opinion that qabbalah is much older than the middle ages, and may in fact go back to the time that the Torah was written, as I personally believe that qabbalistic symbolism is found throughout the Bible- in both the Old and New Testaments, and that many passages of the Bible cannot be understood except for in qabbaltic context and in the symbolic language that can be found in the qabbalah. It should also be mentioned that some scholars see elements of qabalah in the works of the Essenes and in other early Apocryphal texts. Though not called "qabbalah", we can certainly see in the hieroglyphs of ancient Egypt the idea that a picture can take on multiple layers of meaning- with each Egyptian letter not only being the pictorial image of a thing, but also in some cases having multiple meanings including numeric. We also know that certain Hebrew letters resemble similar letters in the Egyptian Hieroglyphics. Therefore it is possible that the Hebrews picked up the idea behind this by the Egyptians. Some esoteric traditions have gone further and asserted that Hebrew was the sacred language of the Egyptians, which had been reserved to the Priesthood. There is nothing to prove these assertions one way or another, but it is interesting to speculate on. The Greeks and Phoenicians likewise had letter forms with symbolic association- including numeric, so since it is found throughout the ancient world, it is very hard to track who had the "original idea". We do know that qabbalah was an oral tradition-being passed on mouth to ear, long before qabbaltistic texts were put in writing. Therefore certain texts like the *Sephir Yetzirah* in the Hebrew tradition are hard to date with any certainty. We also know that it has developed and taken on new forms over the centuries.

I believe that the *Sephir Yetzirah* was the fundamental qabbalistic text however- at least related to what we will be exploring in this book, and in terms of a relation to Freemasonry. As such, reading the *Sephir Yetzirah* and at least having a familiarity with it will be of great value to anyone exploring the ideas presented here after in this book. The version I recommend is by Aryeh Kaplan and is called *Sefer Yetzirah: The Book of Creation In Theory and Practice*, and all quotes herein from the Sefer Yetzirah are from this version. The most important thing to keep in mind with qabbalah is that we are dealing with symbolic language. As such, by not only understanding the symbols themselves, but also the meanings behind them, and how this language relates to us personally, we can in turn be true to what was written over the temple of Apollo in ancient Greece: "know thyself and thou will know the Cosmos and the gods". It is also important to keep in mind that qabbalistic texts like the *Sephir Yetzirah* were never intended to be read like one would read a novel today. Rather, they were challenging texts, full of metaphor and enigma, which were designed to make one think, evaluate, chew and digest in a way in which the result in the end is the reader's greater spiritual growth. Each passage was carefully written to be meditated on, to be discussed, to be debated, and to be explored. Qabbalistic text is a fine dining experience- designed to be savored and explored, and not a fast food eating spree- to be downed and forgotten quickly.

So what of the Biblical origins of these ideas and concepts? Within the Qabbalistic Tree diagram there are 10 "emanations" on the three pillars, which are also called sephiroth, and 22 paths connecting these 10 sephiroth together, thus totaling 32 combinations or expressions of God in creation. Qabbalistic scholars have alluded to the fact that the 32 paths are suggested in the Torah by the 32 times that God's name "Elohim" appears in the account of creation in the first chapter of Genesis. In this account, the expression "God said" appears 10 times, and these are the ten sayings with which the world was created. The ten sayings seem to have correlation with the ten sephiroth on the qabbalstic tree diagram, and alluded to by the *Sephir Yetzirah*, the *Sephir Bahir*, and the *Zohar*. The first saying is spoken of in the verse, "In the beginning God created the Heaven and the Earth" (Genesis 1:1). Even though "God said" does not appear here, it is implied and understood to be associated with this aspect- especially due to the fact that most of the religions of the ancient world associated the beginning of creation with a word, and qabbalistic texts reinforce this idea. Likewise, in the New Testament we are taught: "In the beginning was the word…" within the beginning of the Gospel of John.

The other 22 times that God's name appears in this account seem to match the 22 letters of the Hebrew aleph-beth (alphabet) and by extension the 22 paths. The three times in which the expression "God Made" appears correlate with the three "mother letters" of aleph, mem, and shin (as defined by the *Sephir Yetzirah*). The seven repetitions of "God saw" correlate with the seven "double letters" (called double due to their hard and soft sound)- which are Beth, Gimmel, Dalet, Kaf, Peh, Resh, and Tav. The remaining 12 names correlate with the 12 single (or elemental or simple) letters- which are Heh, Vau, Zayin, Chet, Tet, Yod, Lamed, Nun, Samekh, Eyin, Tzadi, Qof.

I personally believe that there is a correlation as well between which Hebrew letter is associated with each of the actual creation steps- based on what the Hebrew letter is said to be (or be associated with) and correlating it with the action taking place. For example, when "God *made* the beasts of the field", the outline provided above would dictate that this act of creation corresponds with one of the mother Hebrew letters (Aleph, Mem or Shin). I believe that this particular command of creation corresponds specifically with Aleph, since "aleph" means "ox" and its shape kind of looks like the head of an ox or bull. This would of course be a "beast of the field". A similar shape of this letter and association with an ox or bull can also be found in the letter forms of other early cultures.

If we examine another "mother letter"- the letter "Shin", this letter is associated with fire (according to the *Sephir Yetzirah*), and is composed of three of the Hebrew letter "Yod", which is a point with lines going down to a base that connects them all. I feel that this corresponds with "God *made* two luminaries"- as God divides himself into two other points of manifestation. Along this idea, it should be pointed out that the Hebrew letter "Yod" is a point and the letter from which all the other Hebrew letters derive from, and as such, it is a good starting point as a manifestation of God extending Himself. The final "made" phrase in Genesis is "God *made* the firmament"- which would be associated with the Hebrew letter Mem and water. The "firmament" has also been translated as "the waters", so this correlation seems to almost be self explanatory. Another example of a Hebrew letter association with the act of creation taking place may be with the Hebrew letter "Nun"- meaning "fish" and its association in my mind with "God *created* great whales" within the list of 12 single letters. The Hebrew letter Tzaddi is associated with a fish hook, which I came to associate with "God placed them in the firmament"- much like a fish hook is placed in water. Below is a table which shows these correlations with each Hebrew letter, which I have developed from my meditations on the subject. Though the general idea of association has been presented in many books on qabbalah, I have never personally seen a correlation list like this, in which the letters clearly and symbolically associate with each creation act- based on what the letter represents. To my knowledge, this may be the first published list to associate specific acts of creation with specific letters, based on what each letter represents.

Mothers

א	Ox	God made the bests of the field
ש	Tooth	God made two luminaries
מ	Water	God made the firmament

Doubles

ב	House	God saw all that he had made
ג	Camel	God saw that it was good
ד	Door	God saw that it was good
כ	Bent Hand	God saw that it was good
פ	Mouth	God saw that it was good
ר	Head	God saw that it was good
ת	Cross	God saw the light that it was good

Simples/Elementals

ה	Window	God blessed them, be fruitul and multiply
ו	Nail/hook	God created man
ז	Weapon	God called the light day
ח	Fence	God divided between light and darkness
ט	Snake	God called the dry land earth
י	Hand	God said, behold I have given you
ל	Ox Goad	In the form of God He created him
נ	Fish	God created great whales
ס	Prop	God called the firmanent Heaven
ע	Eye	God blessed them
צ	Fish Hook	God placed them in the firmament
ק	Back of Head	And the spirit of God hovered

Sefirot

כתר	In the beginning	God created
הכמה	God said	Let there be light
בינה	God said	Let there be a frimament
הסד	God said	Let the waters be gathered
גבורה	God said	Let the earth be vegetated
תפארת	God said	Let there be luminaries
נצח	God said	Let the waters swarm
הוד	God said	Let the earth bring forth animals
יסוד	God said	Let us make man
מלכות	God said	Be fruitful and multiply

Above: Acts of creation associated with Hebrew letters.

On the Qabbalistic Tree there are attributes associated with each sephirot- or sphere of influence. Going from the top of the Tree and working down, these have been traditionally identified as (1) Crown or Knowledge (Kether), (2) Wisdom (Chochma), (3) Intelligence or Understanding (Binah), (4) Grace, Mercy or Greatness (Chesed), (5) Judgement, Fear or Strength (Geburah or sometimes "Pechad"), (6) Beauty (Tipereth), (7) Victory (Netzach), (8) Glory or Splendor (Hod), (9) Foundation or Power (Yesod), and (10) Kingdom (Malkuth). (See below).

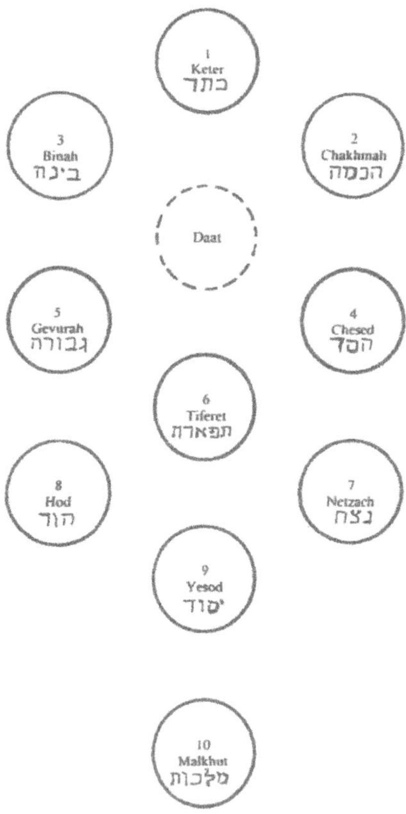

These associations of sephiroth are mentioned by Qabbalistic scholars as related to the Torah with the following:

"I have filled him with the spirit of God, with *Wisdom*, with *Understanding*, and with *Knowledge*"- (Exodus 31:3). (I have italicized the words associated with the top three sephiroth).

"With *Wisdom*, God established the earth, and with *Understanding*, He established the heavens, and with His *Knowledge*, the depths were broken up"- (Proverbs 3:19,20).

"With *Wisdom* a house is built, with *Understanding* it is established, and with *Knowledge* its rooms are filled"- (Proverbs 24:3,4).

In Chronicles 29:11 the bottom seven sephiroth are outlined (I listed the sephiroth's number next to its association in the passage): "Yours O God are the *Greatness* (4), the *Strength* (5), the *Beauty* (6), the *Victory* (7), and the *Splendor* (8), for *All* (9) in heaven and in earth; yours O God is the *Kingdom* (10)".

In the Christian tradition, the Lord's Prayer likewise ends with: "for Thou are the Kingdom (10), the Power (9), and the Glory (8) forever and ever."

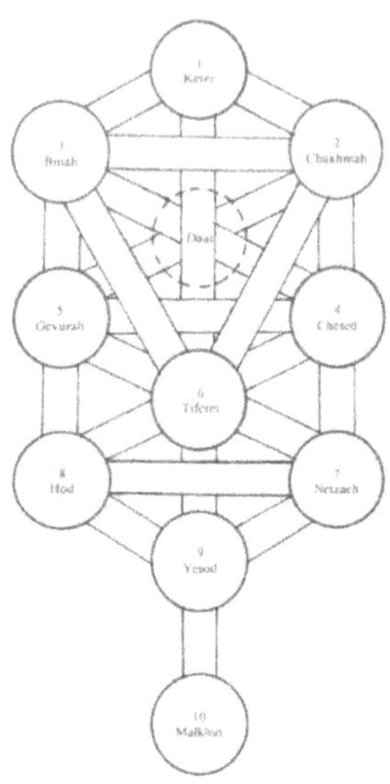

So to reiterate, between the 10 emanations or sephiroth, and the 22 paths and/or letters, there are a total of 32 combinations. Again, some traditions recognize a hidden 11th sephiroth- called Daath, which would bring the total number of manifestations to 33. Perhaps also interesting is the fact the in Hebrew the number 32 is written "Lamed-Beth". This spells "lev"- the Hebrew word for "heart". The Torah is seen as the heart of creation, and as Freemasons, it is interesting that this is where our consciousness is first drawn when we first enter the lodge room as an Entered Apprentice. This is reinforced later when we are asked "where were you first prepared to be made a Mason?" This is one of the esoteric keys behind what the great Masonic and Martinist initiates of Louis Claude de St. Martin and Papus referred to as "the way of the heart". The first letter of the Torah is Beth of "Bereshit"- "in the beginning". The last letter of the Torah is "Lamed" of "Yisrael"- "Israel". Together these two letters spell out "lev"- "heart", and associate with the number 32. (This aspect of using the first and last letters of words to form other words is part of a qabbalistic science called *Notarikon*). Scottish Rite Freemasons revere 32 as the culmination of degrees that any brother can receive in that system- with an honorary 33rd degree (much like a hidden 33rd manifestation on the qabbalistic tree). Some have likewise made association with this number 32 and the 32 levels on the human spinal column- with the 33rd level being the brain that rests on top of it. Within the Christian tradition, we also see 33 associated with the number of years of Jesus' mission on earth.

Table Showing the 33 Sectioned Vertebrae with Correspondences

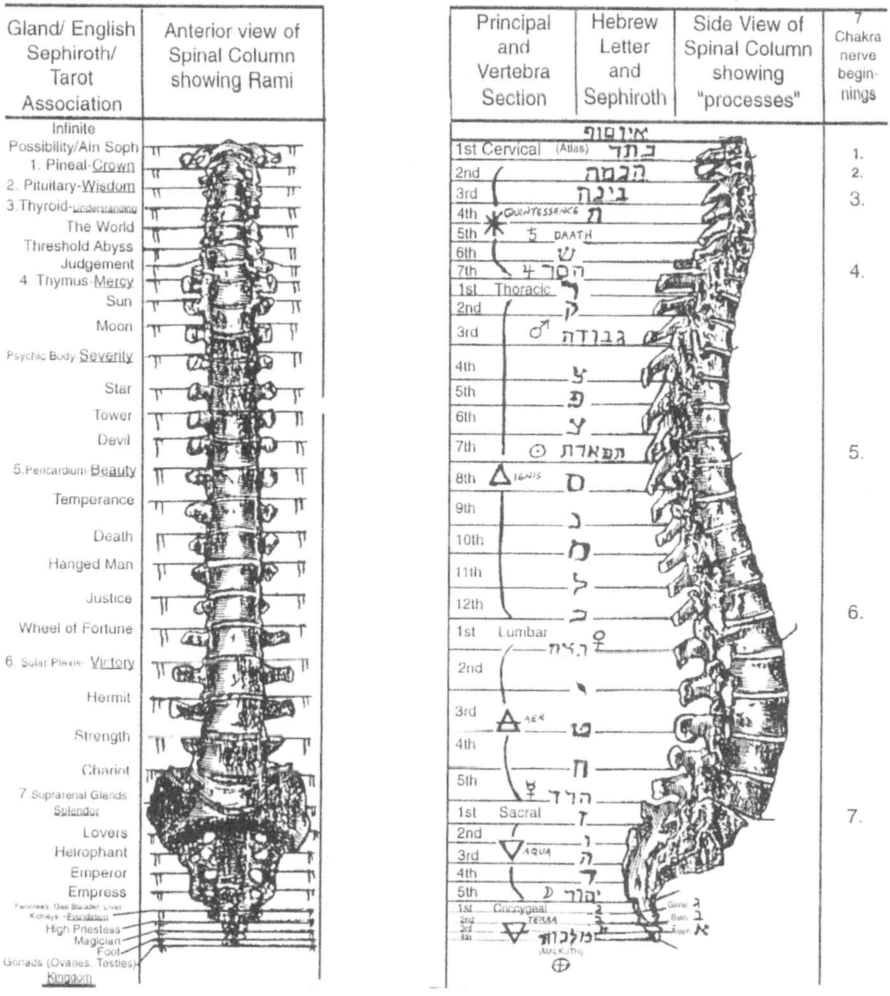

Gland/ English Sephiroth/ Tarot Association	Anterior view of Spinal Column showing Rami	Principal and Vertebra Section	Hebrew Letter and Sephiroth	Side View of Spinal Column showing "processes"	7 Chakra nerve beginnings
Infinite Possibility/Ain Soph			אין סוף		
1. Pineal-Crown		1st Cervical (Atlas)	כתר		1.
2. Pituitary-Wisdom		2nd	חכמה		2.
3. Thyroid-Understanding		3rd	בינה		3.
The World		4th ✱ Quintessence	ת		
Threshold Abyss		5th	♄ Daath		
Judgement		6th	ש		
4. Thymus-Mercy		7th	♃ חסד		4.
Sun		1st Thoracic	ר		
Moon		2nd	ק		
Psychic Body-Severity		3rd	♂ גבורה		
Star		4th	צ		
Tower		5th	פ		
Devil		6th	ע		
5. Pericardium-Beauty		7th	☉ תפארת		5.
Temperance		8th △ Ignis	ס		
Death		9th	נ		
Hanged Man		10th	מ		
Justice		11th	ל		
Wheel of Fortune		12th	כ		
6. Solar Plexus- Victory		1st Lumbar	♀ נצח		6.
Hermit		2nd	י		
Strength		3rd △ Aer	ט		
Chariot		4th	ח		
7 Suprarenal Glands- Splendor		5th	☿ הוד		
Lovers		1st Sacral	ז		7.
Heirophant		2nd	ו		
Emperor		3rd ▽ Aqua	ה		
Empress		4th	ד		
Pancreas, Gall Bladder, Liver Kidneys -Foundation		5th	☽ יסוד		
High Priestess		1st Coccygeal	ג	Gimel ג	
Magician		2nd Terra	ב	Beth ב	
Fool		3rd	א	Aleph א	
Gonads (Ovaries, Testies) Kingdom		4th	מלכות (Malkuth) ⊕		

Also of notice regarding the Qabbalistic Tree diagram is the fact that it has three principle horizontal paths, said to separate the tree into four worlds or divisions. The emphasis of these three paths are what associate the Tree diagram with Jacob's Ladder- the three principle rungs of which represented faith, hope, and charity…which is an important symbol in Freemasonry. The four worlds on the tree were said to represent various levels of human awareness and consciousness which may be summarized as material, psychological, spiritual, and divine. In the qabbalah, they were referred to as Assiah (physical world of fabrication), Yetzirah (formative world), Briah (creation world), and Atziluth (emanation world). All progress on the Tree and within initiation rites has been directed at taking someone in the physical world of objective awareness (Assiah) and gradually moving them up through the other three worlds towards union with the emanation world of God (Atziluth) by passing through the three principle stages or initiations. Therefore initiation took one out of the material world and began progression through the three main stages- represented by the three principle rungs on the tree that divided the upper three worlds. In Isaiah 43:7 we see these levels emphasized: "All that is called in My Name, for My Emanation (Atziluth), I have created it (Briah), I have formed it (Yetzirah), and I have made it (Assiah)". Within the Gnostic schools, such levels of awareness were likewise important in initiation rites, and were catalogued as Hylic, Psychic, Pneumatic, and Gnostic. Some have taken this a step further and associated with the various levels of consciousness as classified by an EEG- primarily being Beta waves (objective phase of attention), Alpha waves (calmed and relaxed subjective state), Theta waves (intermediate state of consciousness between subconscious and subjective consciousness), and Delta waves (dreamless sleep of deep subconscious also found at approaching death). It has also been catalogued as Objective awareness, Subjective awareness, Subconscious activity, and Cosmic Consciousness (or the deep state of consciousness which connects us with all consciousness of creation). Some teachers of Qabbalah have likewise associated the three levels with grades of the soul, known as "nephesh"- or vital principle which inhabits and governs all of the organic or material body and lower psyche, "ruah"- or spirit and seat of the will (generally constituting individual human personality), and "neshamah" or soul proper (the seat of the spiritual element in each human and the ability to reason). Spiritual development involves degrees of Mastery within each of these three principle stages.

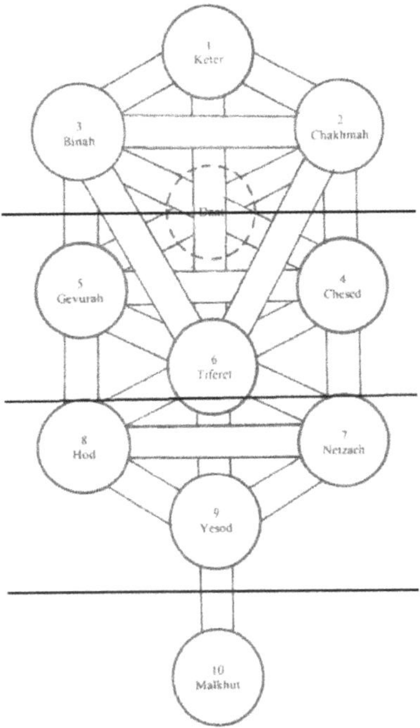

Some qabbalists have taken this a step further and asserted that there is a separate tree of 10 emanations for each particular stage of the four stages of development. Looked at in this light, there would be a total of 40 different spheres of manifestation that each initiate would have to work through before exploring every sphere of the qabbalistic tree. Qabbalistic scholars have looked to the number 40 in the Bible as alluding to this aspect- which we can certainly see with the wandering of 40 years in the desert, or 40 days and 40 nights of Noah in the great flood, and other areas that it shows up. In summary however, the first level was always an aspect that everyone alive has been incarnated into. Therefore the initiation into it is birth. However the following three levels required levels of initiation and mastery to achieve- according to the traditional schools. Others have interpreted the number 40 in these contexts to representing spending 4 days meditating on each sephirot of the tree- and examining each one from the aspect of one of the elements: earth, water, air, and fire, before moving on to the next sephirot. The result would be a total of 40 days. In this capacity, each element represented a quality or state of being.

Freemasonry will recognize the three principle levels as being associated with the three principle symbolic degrees of Entered Apprentice, Fellow Craft, and Master Mason, and will relate them as well to the divisions of King Solomon's Temple: the outer porch, the middle chamber, and the Sanctum Sanctorum or Holy of Hollies. Some researchers have likewise advanced the idea that the three principle levels of initiation, as found on the Qabbalistic Tree, represent the various levels of acquiring the knowledge of Deity. Manly P. Hall, in his book *The Wisdom of the Knowing Ones*, has this to say on the subject:

"Broadly speaking, both Eastern and Western mystics recognized three levels of knowledge and three ways in which it can be attained. By knowledge, we mean the sacred truths of religion and philosophy. The first way of attainment is by study and research. It assumes no extraordinary capacity on the part of the truth seeker, except sincerity and a reasonably well cultivated intellect.... The second way by which enlightenment can be advanced is called spiritual intuition. This is the stimulation of the inner resources of the individual by which he comes to sense or feel the reality of his own spiritual life... The third way is described as "standing face to face with reality." It is the refinement and amplification of the inner life to the degree that spirituality is a complete experience...This may be considered an illumination or mystical experience... These three levels can be paralleled with the three degrees of knowledge accepted by Kabalists. Using the Temple of Solomon as the symbol of the House of Wisdom, they recognize it as divisible into three parts... These in turn were likened to the three degrees of spiritual instruction: the (first was the) Torah, or the law of Moses, (and) was for those who studied and sought to inform themselves concerning the will of God. The (second was the) Mishnah, which was called the soul of the law, was for those who possessed intuitive power and were able to sense the mystery beneath the literal exposition as set forth in the Torah. The third part was the Kabala, the truly esoteric doctrine, containing the secret instructions by which the person could attain direct participation in the essence of God."[1]

We will explore these divisions in more detail in a future chapter, but for now it is enough to recognize them and understand their place on the Qabbaltic Tree which has been generally outlined. I would also recommend Kirk McKnulty's excellent book "The Way of the Craftsmen", which examines these various levels of qabbalah in detail, and relates them to the degrees of Freemasonry and the journey that each Masonic initiate takes through the degrees.

As mentioned, the Qabbalistic Tree is likewise composed of three vertical pillars. The two outside pillars represented opposite forces that are reconciled in the middle pillar. Some associations with these two outside pillars are strength and beauty, strength and establishment, severity and mildness, and other opposites of human conception- which become reconciled in the third element- that of the middle pillar of wisdom. The two outside pillars ultimately

1-Hall, Manly P, *The Wisdom of the Knowing Ones*, pg. 70-71.

represent all opposite forces of nature, and borrowing from the Eastern traditions, we may call them Yin and Yang. As mentioned previously, within the frame work of King Solomon's Temple, they were represented by the two pillars on the outer porch, and as opposites, we may recognize them as the black and white checkered pavement of Masonic instruction. The initiate stands between the two pillars- reconciling the opposites. The events in the degree initiations of Freemasonry make it clear that the first degree emphasizes one side of the body, the second degree emphasizes the other side, and the third degree balances everything out. Therefore the pillars are part of each initiate, and the Master learns to balance them in themselves. The Tree then, becomes a model of ourselves, and a model of our Lodge /Temple.

Esoteric tradition has named this trinity of opposites that reconcile into a third point of manifestation the "Law of the Triangle", and in this way, esoterically it can be said that 1+1=3. Reconciling in the middle pillar is one of the goals of Mastery in qabbalah, and it should be noted that this middle pillar is composed of the 1st, the 6th, the 9th, and the 10th sephirot- being Kether, Tipereth, Yesod, and Malkuth respectively. If we add these together: 1+6+9+10 we get a sum of 26. This number, 26, is also the sum found within the Hebrew name of God as YHVH- which numerically is 10+5+6+5 according to qabbalistic doctrine of gematria that will be covered in Chapter 3. Therefore to walk the middle path of the middle pillar, is to walk in harmony with the wisdom of God- harmonizing all the forces and opposites, and using them as tools as opposed to obstacles. Masonic scholars have likewise been quick to point out over the centuries that if we take the Hebrew words representing the pillars as "beauty", "strength", and "wisdom"- which are "Gomer", "Oz", and "Dabar" respectively in Hebrew, the first letter of each spells the word G-O-D. Therefore one of the keys to living in harmony with God's creation is to find balance, which is likewise dramatically illustrated within the three degrees of

Freemasonry. It should be mentioned that some qabbalistic scholars associate the two outer pillars with the "Tree of Life", and the middle pillar with the "Tree of Knowledge". The Tree of Life therefore teaches the dualities of life, and the Tree of Knowledge masters this knowledge and utilizes it in wisdom.

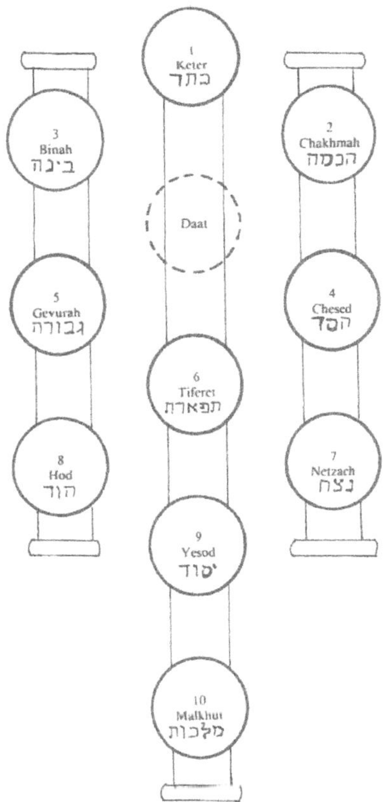

So in summary, the Qabbalistic Tree is composed of 10 sephiroth, 22 paths between these sephiroth (represented by the 22 letters of the Hebrew alphabet), three pillars, and four worlds. Every person alive exists on the lowest world, but initiation and consciousness illumination are the keys to access to the upper three worlds- each of which brings one closer to understanding the creation of God and by extension, God Himself. In many ways, meditation on these qabbalistic concepts correlates perfectly with the Hermetic concept of "as above, so below; as within, so without" inscribed in the Hermetic texts and the famed Emerald Tablet of Hermes. This same idea is stated in the Zohar which says: "Everything is connected with everything, right through to the nethermost end of all the links of the chain, and the true essence of God is both above and below, in the heavens and on earth, and nothing exists apart from it." Such symbolism is reinforced with the globes on top of the pillars in Masonic ritual, and it implies a profound idea: that God is in us and we are in God. Therefore the Qabbalistic Tree not only represents the stages of our consciousness, but the philosophical structure of Universal Creation, and by extension, it also represents the human body itself. Meditation long enough on one aspect naturally leads to the others- with everything connected to everything else, as the Zohar says. Therefore even though these concepts may at first seem strange and ambiguous, it is important to keep them in mind as we progress. In the next chapter, it is important to examine and re-examine the correlations of the Hebrew letters on the paths of the Qabbalistic Tree, as well as the association of the planets with each sephirot. As will be revealed, there is a good chance that what has become the standard model in the western traditions over the centuries is wrong- and that there is another possible combination which makes perfect sense in symbolic clarity, and which has been alluded to in Masonic ritual and tradition for centuries as well.

Chapter 2: A New Examination

The Qabbalistic Tree has always been composed of the ten main emanations, or sephirot, and the 22 paths that connect between them. Traditionally the paths have been assigned to the 22 Hebrew letters by taking the first path on top and assigning it to the first Hebrew letter Aleph, the second path on top and assigning it to the second Hebrew letter Beth, and the just working its way down the tree assigning each path to each consecutive letter as it gradually moves down. This has been the standard accepted association for the paths. The Sephirot on the other hand were generally assigned to the seven planets of antiquity and the Earth, starting with Malkuth (Kingdom) at the bottom representing Earth, Yesod (Foundation) representing the Moon, Hod (Glory) representing Mercury, Netzach (Victory) representing Venus, Tipereth (Beauty) representing the Sun, Geburah (Judgement) representing Mars, Chesed (Grace) representing Jupiter, and then arose the great debate on where to put Saturn.

Traditionally Saturn was generally placed in Binah (Intelligence)...however in doing so the result is it is not with the other six planets on the lower part of the tree that are usually associated with the days of creation that come out of the trinity. To solve this problem, other schools have placed Saturn in the hidden Sephirot of Daath. This tends to make more sense from a symbolic standpoint, and we see it alluded to on the hexagram on Hermetic Rose-Cross that the Hermetic Order of the Golden Dawn has used. When place in this position, it remains below the creation trinity of the upper three sephirot and it falls on the middle pillar along with the Sun, Moon, and Earth. From a gravitational standpoint, it is in fact the Moon, Sun, and Saturn which anchor the Earth. Saturn was also associated with Father Time, and by extension the Grim

Reaper and death. Some have suggested that it is no coincidence that "death" and "Daath" sound so much alike- as "Daath" is as far as your consciousness can climb while incarnated in a body before having to die and cross the threshold to the upper trinity. According to some qabbalistic schools you must cross through this abyss of death before most can access the upper three sephirot. (If not literally, then at least some form of symbolic death of your old self- like in initiation…which has resonance with the third degree in Freemasonry). The astrological symbol for Saturn is the scythe, which cuts things down. The same reaper symbol is always depicted hidden in his cloak, much like Daath is the hidden sephirot. Others have suggested that the Sun is a great faucet of life force in our solar system and Saturn is the great drain for the same energy, which is why only the bodies between the Sun and Saturn were recognized in astrology in antiquity. (However these happen to also be the only bodies that can be seen by the naked eye). Other qabbalists have seen in this model a metaphor for the alchemical process of turning lead into gold- as lead was associated with Saturn and gold was associated with the Sun. Therefore it seems somewhat fitting that Saturn, the Sun, the Moon, and Earth are all on the same pillar.

Some have taken this a step further and found allusions to it in Hiram's memorial, as found in Freemasonry- which has Father Time (Saturn), counting golden locks (sun), as the maiden holds the silver urn (moon), which contains the ashes of Hiram (earth). Again, I don't whole heartedly agree with these interpretations, but I point them out in case others find validity in them for their own researches. If this is the case, then we can see two Solomon's seals interlaced on the Qabbalistic Tree- with the center of one being Tiferet and the center of the other being Daat. I should also mention that according to some doctrines, the sun is a doorway for a higher dimensional etheric force and Saturn is the drain for this same energy, which ties in with ancient astrology only using the seven planetary bodies between the Sun and Saturn. Recent photos of the poles of Saturn have shown that there is a hexagon pattern that is regularly formed by the clouds at the north pole of Saturn, and there is nothing in current models of planetary physics that can explain this- unless, of course, we apply a topographical model to it figuring in the geometry of higher dimensions, in which case we would expect to see a hexagon at the poles. This suggests that Saturn may be a drain, or indwelling source for some higher dimensional energy. The internal geometry behind a hexagon, is of course, a Solomon's Seal- or six pointed star. So this may provide further light on the idea that these ancient truths may hold the keys to future science....

However good either of these two explanations sound as the possible associations between the planets and the sephiroth, there are in fact other interpretations from other schools of thought which are in fact older. I am in no way trying to suggest that the above interpretations are valid or not valid- and there are entire schools of thought based on their respective validity. However there are other ways of associating them which I think may match better and of which certainly tie better into the rituals of Freemasonry. For example, the alchemist Anton Kircher diagramed them out differently in *Edipus Egyptiacus*- as shown on the next page.

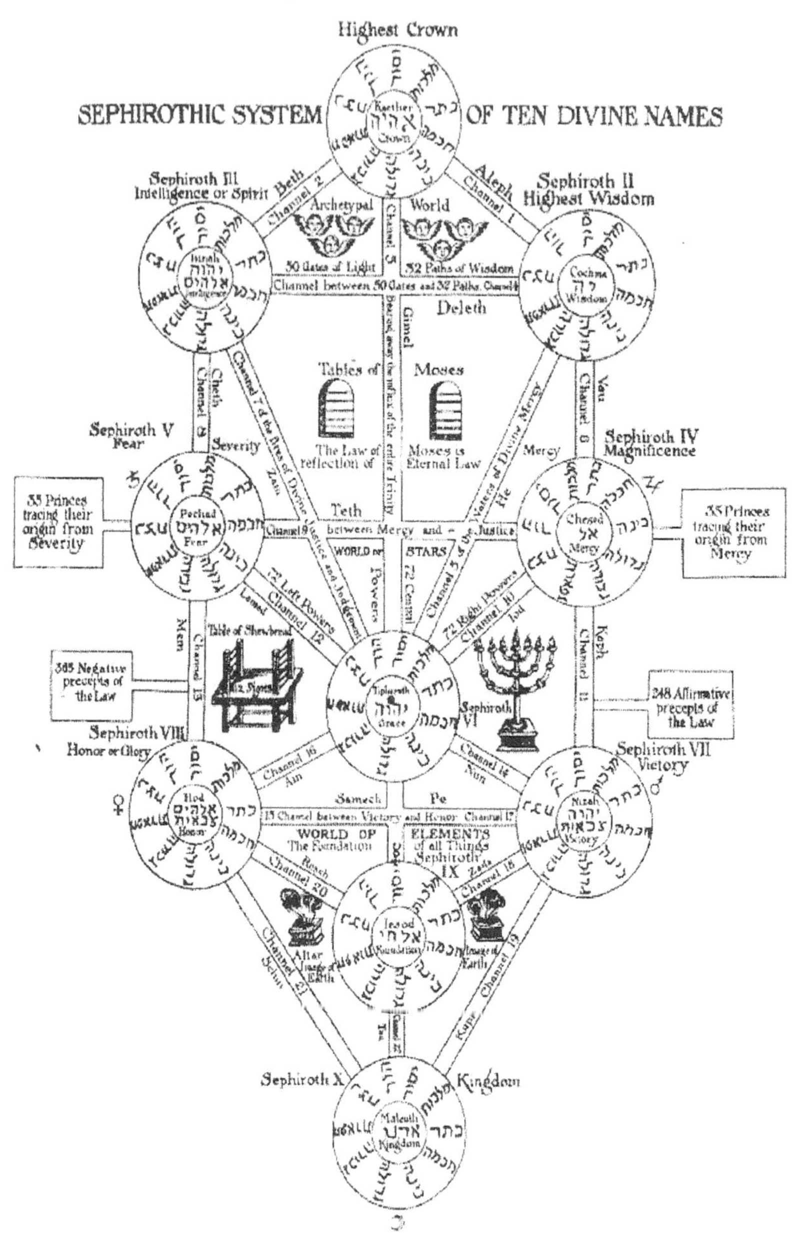
Highest Crown
SEPHIROTHIC SYSTEM OF TEN DIVINE NAMES
Sephiroth III
Intelligence or Spirit
Sephiroth II
Highest Wisdom
Archetypal World
50 Gates of Light
32 Paths of Wisdom
Deleth
Tables of Moses
Sephiroth V
Fear
Severity
Mercy
Sephiroth IV
Magnificence
The Law of reflection of
Moses is Eternal Law
35 Princes tracing their origin from Severity
35 Princes tracing their origin from Mercy
Teth
between Mercy and Justice
WORLD OF STARS
72 Left Powers
72 Right Powers
Table of Shewbread
365 Negative precepts of the Law
248 Affirmative precepts of the Law
Sephiroth VI
Sephiroth VIII
Honor or Glory
Sephiroth VII
Victory
Samech
Pe
WORLD OF The Foundation
ELEMENTS of all Things
Sephiroth IX
Altar
Image of Earth
Sephiroth X
Kingdom

In this interpretation, we can clearly see the letters of the Hebrew alphabet that are assigned to each path as starting at the top of the tree and going down. However in Kircher's diagram, the earth is not represented at all on a sephirot. Rather, Malkuth is represented by the Moon, Yesod by Mercury, Netzach by Mars, Hod by Venus, Tipereth by the Sun, Chesed by Jupiter, and Geburah (here called Pechad) by Saturn. This places them all under the upper trinity of Sephirot without having to use the secret 11th Sepiroth of Daath as a possible place for Saturn. From an alchemical standpoint, this model of planets in relation to sephirot actually works best, as each planet can be associated with its noble metal: (Saturn to lead, Jupiter to tin, the Sun to gold, Mars to iron, Venus to copper, Mercury to quicksilver, and the Moon to silver). Likewise, each metal and planet had association with certain qualities- both virtues and vices. Earth is not associated by a metal, and therefore in the other potential versions of the tree listed above, the bottom sphere of Malkuth would be missing a metal. What is significant in this Kircher diagram is that the middle pillar gets formed by the Moon, Mercury, and the Sun. This is significant from a Masonic perspective, because Mercury was likewise associated with the Greek Hermes (the messenger), who was likewise associated with Hiram…who by extension every Master Mason represents. Therefore the middle pillar becomes represented by the Sun, Moon, and Master- which we recognize as the Lesser Lights in Freemasonry. Traditionally alchemical texts have likewise emphasized Apollo (the Sun), Diana (the Moon) and Mercury as particularly featured together on alchemical diagrams. Other alchemical diagrams likewise emphasize the sun, moon, and mercury together (as shown on next page from the frontpiece of *Fasciculus Chemicus* translated and published by Elias Ashmole in 1650). You will also notice in it the pillars emphasized. (Elias Ashmole is famed for being one of the first English Freemasons).

Astra
regunt
homines
Quod est superius est sicut inferius
Mercurio-
philus
Anglicus
London
Printed for Richard Mynne

Mercury likewise is usually depicted holding his staff at its base, in the same relative position that the sephirot associated with Mercury would be if the staff becomes the middle pillar on the qabbalistic tree. In Masonic ritual in most jurisdictions of the United States, the Junior and Senior Deacons both carry a rod like Mercury, and one has the sun on it and the other the moon. They are messengers, like Mercury was to the gods, and representing Mercury it is significant that one has a rod going to the moon and the other has a rod going to the sun- the two sephirot that would be below and above Mercury. In some Masonic jurisdictions around the world, the Deacons actually have Mercury depicted on their rods as opposed to the sun and moon.

I will also mention is passing that in antiquity each of the seven planets ruled one of the seven days of the week and the seven liberal arts and sciences. Another thing significant with this location for the planets is that the seven days of creation become outlined below the upper trinity. This layout reinforces the Biblical narrative for the days of creation along with everything else.

It is for these reasons, and several others which I will bring to light as we continue our journey, that I believe Kircher's association of the planets and the sephirot is correct. I do not think that Kircher's association of the Hebrew letters with the paths is correct however, and I am even willing to believe that this was put in as a blind that has stuck in esoteric literature. As will be shown as we go, the symbolic degrees of Freemasonry offer clues as to the correct location of these associations, and the Masonic degrees and alchemical texts validate Kircher's association of the planets to the sephirot. Therefore from this point forward, we will use his planetary associations for the sephirot.

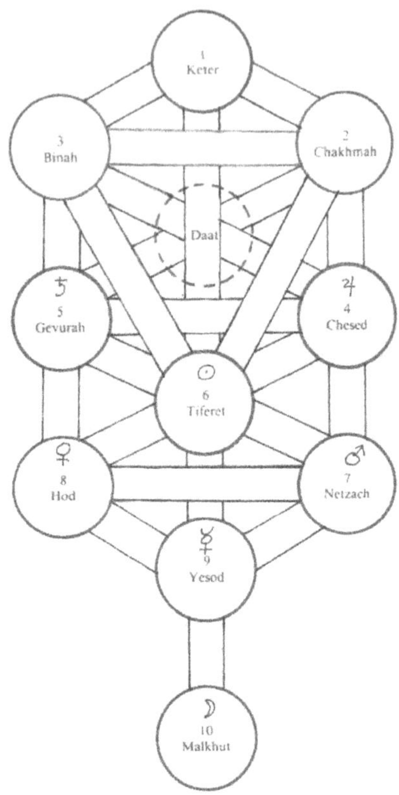

Now we need to examine the paths that compose the tree. As mentioned, the traditional designation has been to lay out the letters from top to bottom, going from the first Hebrew letter Aleph and working our way down in order. Many schools of qabbalistic thought have come up with all kinds of interpretations behind why this order for the letters work, some of which sound somewhat reasonable, and some of which sound utterly forced in my opinion. This order has never seemed correct to me however, for a number of reasons. First and foremost, we are taught in traditional qabbalistic texts like the *Sephir Yetzirah* that there are three mother letters, seven double letters, and twelve simple letters. By more than coincidence in my mind, there are also happens to be three horizontal paths on the qabbalistic tree, seven vertical paths, and twelve diagonal paths. This would almost imply that the three "mother" letters should in fact go on the three horizontal bars, the seven "double letters" should go on the seven vertical bars, and the twelve "simple" letters should go on the twelve diagonal bars. If this is the case, then the next thing we need to ask ourselves is which Hebrew letter goes on which path? The answer to this question is actually easier than might be expected, and it reveals some startling associations which we find reflected in the degrees of Freemasonry.

First off, the easiest letters to place would be the seven "double letters". They are called double because they have the hard and soft sound, but maybe they are also double because the vertical path they are meant to be on connects to a sephirot of the same association. Since each of these seven Hebrew letters are ruled by a planet, if we use Kircher's planetary association for the sephirot, then it becomes very clear which Hebrew letter should connect with which sephirot. By this association, Resh (associated with Saturn) connects with Judgment (Geburah) also associated with Saturn, Kaf (associated with Venus) connects with Glory (Hod) also associated with Venus, Tav (associated with Jupiter) connects with Mercy (Chesed) also associated with Jupiter, Gimel (associated with Mars) connects with Victory (Netzach) also associated with Mars, Dalet (associated with the Sun) connects with Beauty (Tipereth) also associated with the Sun, Peh (associated with Mercury) connects with Foundation (Yesod) also associated with Mercury, and Beth (associated with the moon) connects with Kingdom (Malkuth) also associated with the Moon. This seems to be a natural flow of energy with the Hebrew letter associated with a planet flowing into the sephirot ruled by the same planet, which makes a great deal of sense symbolically. The path of the planet leads to the planet. There is no forced interpretation.

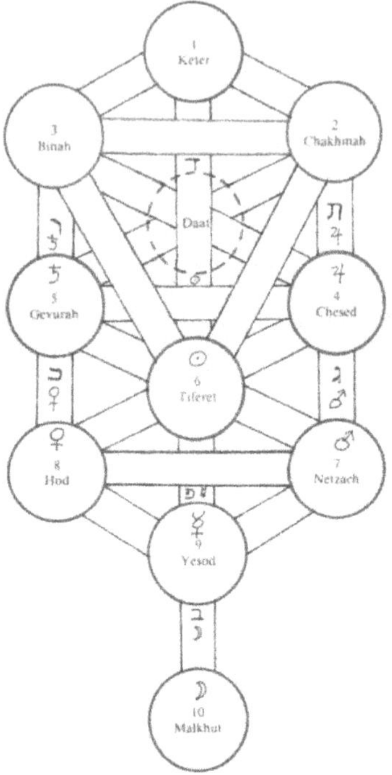

The next set of paths to determine would be the three horizontal paths. There are three mother letters in Hebrew composed of Mem (associated with water), Aleph (associated with air), and Shin (associated with fire). Traditionally the form of the tree of life has been considered both a projection of the human body and a layout of King Solomon's Temple- following the idea that "your body is a temple". It has also been suggested that King Solomon's Temple was laid out like the human to reflect the idea of a resonance between the person and the temple- as above, so below. Such a lay out is also found with the cathedrals of Notre Dame and many ancient Egyptian temples, assumingly due to the fact that they derived from similar esoteric tradition. By this model then, the abdomen would be associated with water- since that is where all digestive and liquid functions of the body primarily take place.

This is likewise the area where the watery, or liquid elements of the body are primarily stored. Air, on the other hand, would be associated with the chest- since this is the area of the lungs where air is taken in to the body. As the vital principle in air is taken into the lungs of the chest, it is then absorbed in the blood and pumped around the body. Fire would be associated with the head, since the brain works off of electrical impulses to motivate the nervous system- which is a kind of fire force. "Shin" also has the Hebrew meaning of "tooth", which would obviously put it in the head. By this reasoning, the lowest horizontal path on the qabbalistic tree would be associated with water and the Hebrew letter Mem, the horizontal path in the middle would be associated with air and Aleph, and the upper most horizontal path would be associated with fire and the Hebrew letter Shin. The rungs of the ladder going up our tree then become water, air, and fire as we progress higher.

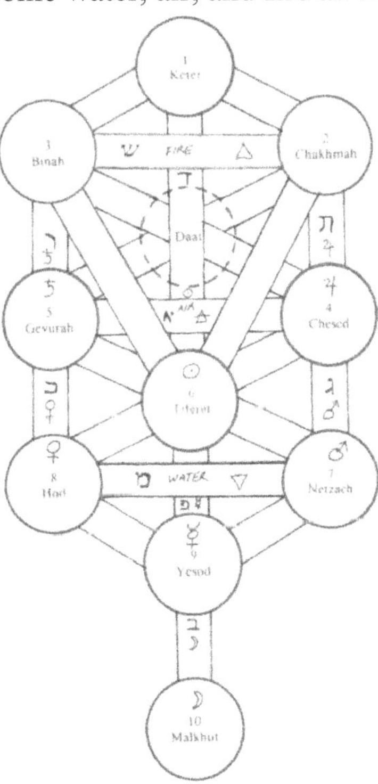

This association actually makes a lot of sense from an initiation standpoint, and traditionally the initiate in the mystery schools would go through various levels of baptism as they progressed upwards in advancement- moving closer to the source of Deity. The first stage was a baptism by water, the second a baptism by air, and the last a baptism by fire- progressing from the most dense to most ethereal element. Water represented mastery over the emotions, air represented mastery over the intellect, and fire represented mastery over the will and a connection with the divine. By using this layout on the qabbalistic tree, the initiate actually must move up and past each of these levels as he moves closer to the upper divine realms. He attempts to achieve a reintegration with Deity after having experienced a symbolic fall into matter. If we look at this in association with King Solomon's Temple- in particular in relation to Masonic initiation, when moving from Yesod to Tipereth the initiate must cross the path of water, and we may see this area as the outer porch of King Solomon's Temple, and the penalty of the Entered Apprentice. Next as the initiate moves into Tipereth, the two pillars on either side come into view, and the initiate must cross the path of air as he dwells in the middle chamber of King Solomon's Temple. We see this illustrated when the Fellow Craft stands between the two pillars, and who has a penalty associated with air. He also stands in the center of the seven lower spheres, traditionally associated with the seven liberal arts and sciences. Finally, in order to enter into the Sanctum Sanctorum, or Holy of Holies of King Solomon's Temple, and become a Master, the initiate must cross the horizontal path of fire. It is not coincidence, in my opinion that this is the exact order of the penalties in Masonic ritual, with the Entered Apprentice being exposed to water, the Fellow Craft being exposed to air, and the Master Mason being exposed to fire. Should we doubt this at all, let us remember the Master Mason's grip, in which the hand in placed in the shape of the Hebrew letter Shin. In fact both Jewish and Eastern Orthodox Priests make blessings with their hand in this shape because it does represent the active force of fire, and of course the pass word of the Master Mason relates to fire. (For those non-Masons foolish enough to think they now know the full grip of a Master Mason, I regret to tell you that there is more to it, so you don't know much!) Other people have seen the Shin as represented as well by the three lights about the altar in Masonic symbolism. This progression of water-air-fire likewise follows the steps and stages of alchemy, as outlined in my book *The Alchemical Keys to Masonic Ritual.*

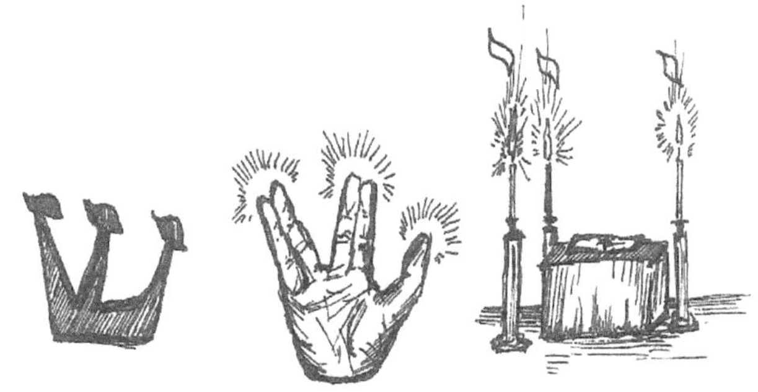

Above: The letter Shin, the hand in Shin, and the Masonic altar.

Some may be asking, "what about earth"? It was implied in the qabbalah that earth did not need to be learned, as everyone is born in a physical body and was attached to it, so therefore everyone knows earth. Each person must quest outside of themselves for understanding into the other levels or aspects of consciousness- represented by water, air, and fire. Even Jesus said, "those who came before me baptized with water and air, but I have come to baptize with fire." However, some schools have depicted another veil as existing before Malkuth, thus forming four veils in all, with each tied to one of the four elements…again very much relating to the veils or gates in King Solomon's Temple and which is later emphasized in the Royal Arch Degree of Freemasonry.

If we accept this order for Shin, Aleph, and Mem on the paths of the tree, not only does it follow the order of initiation, but there are other associations that come into view. First of all, Aleph is placed in the middle of the qabbalistic tree- with one arm of Aleph pointing up and one arm of Aleph pointing down- a fitting spot for being on the chest that maintains the arms. Some have seen the Magician card in the tarot as being associated with Aleph, and he too points with his arms to the above and the below. The letter Aleph being in this position is perfectly placed as balancing the two extremes of water and fire (Men and Shin). In fact, the *Sephir Yetzirah* even alludes to this throughout its text many times suggesting that air is the balance between fire and water- or even that fire and water both emanated as opposite extremes from God's breath (Air). For example, in section 1:12 it says:

"Fire from water
With it He engraved and carved
The Throne of Glory
Serafim, Ophanim, and holy Chayot
And Ministering angels
From these three He founded His dwelling
As it is written:
"He makes His angels of breaths,
His ministers of flaming fire." (Psalms 104:4)

In section 2:1 in the *Sephir Yetzirah*, it says of the mother letters:

"The Three Mothers are Aleph Mem Shin
a pan of merit
a pan of liability
and the tongue of decree deciding between them."
Mem hums, Shin hisses, and Aleph is the Breath of air deciding between them."

In section 3:4 in the *Sephir Yetzirah* this is further emphasized:

"The Mothers, Aleph, Mem, Shin in the Universe are air, water, fire.
Heaven was created from fire.
Earth was created from water.
And air from Breath decides between them."

In section 6:2 in the *Sephir Yetzirah* it is emphasized again:

"Three Mothers: Aleph, Mem, Shin
Air, water, fire.
Fire is above, water is below,
And air of breath is the rule
That decides between them.
And a sign of this thing
Is that fire supports water.
Mem hums, Shin hisses,
And Aleph is the breath of air
That decides between them."

These passages in particular stress that Aleph should balance out Mem and Shin, and therefore be placed between them on the tree. They also plainly state that Shin should be placed "above" in "Heaven" and water should be placed "below" on "earth". In section 3:9 of the Sepher Yetzirah it suggests that the letter Shin should be placed near the crown- which is the top Sephirot of Kether (also associated with the top of the head).

"He made Shin king over fire and He bound a crown to it
and He combined one with another
And with them He formed Heaven in the Universe, Hot in the Year,
And the head in the Soul..."

When we place the three mother letters on the paths as outlined above, the result is, in fact, that Aleph balances out Mem and Shin between them on the tree. So not only does having the three mother letters on the three horizontal paths correspond with qabbalistic texts like the *Sephir Yetzirah*, but it also follows the ancient initiation rites which are also found in Freemasonry, and it follows the layout of the human body. Therefore everything is united, and it becomes clear that it would not make sense to place any other Hebrew letters on these particular paths.

This brings us to our next problem- where do we place the twelve simple letters on the 12 diagonal paths of the tree? Again, the *Sephir Yetzirah* comes to our aid! If we use the qabbalistic tree as a model of the human body, with Shin associated with the horizontal path defining the head, Aleph associated with the horizontal path associated with the chest, and Mem associated with the horizontal path associated with the abdomen, then we also learn that each of the twelve simple letters are associated with various organs of the body. Therefore the organ that each letter is associated with should define for us their location on the tree! If this were not enough, there is another code built into the text that further helps us. Each of the twelve simple letters are likewise associated with a sign of the Zodiac. Therefore it should follow that the diagonal path associated with a Zodiacal sign should likewise come in contact with, or lead to, the planet that traditionally rules it in astrology- (since the paths of the planets go to the sephirot that is associated with the same planet, and these in turn should have influence on the astrological sign traditionally connected with them). Low and behold, to my amazement, not only did I find that if we follow these two clues, they tell us exactly where to place the 12 simple Hebrew letters on the 12 diagonal paths.

צ ♒	Esophagus
ק ♓	Back of Head
ט ♐	Stomach
ל ♎	Gall
י ♍	Left hand
ח ♋	Right Hand

ע ♑	Liver
ו ♉	Right Kidney
ט ♌	Left Kidney
נ ♏	Small Intestine
ז ♊	Left Foot
ה ♈	Right Foot

Hebrew letter and Zodaical sign with part of the body, based on *Sephir Yetzirah.*

For example, Qoph is associated with the back of the head and Pisces, therefore it should be placed connecting Kether (Crown) to Chokmah (Understanding)- which in turn connects to the path of its ruling planet of Jupiter. Tzaddi is associated with the esophagus and Aquarius, and therefore should go the opposite of the back of the head and connect Kether (the Crown) to Binah (Understanding), and it then comes in contact with the vertical path of Saturn which rules Aquarius. Both of these paths, connected with the head, end up residing above the path of Shin- which defines the head.

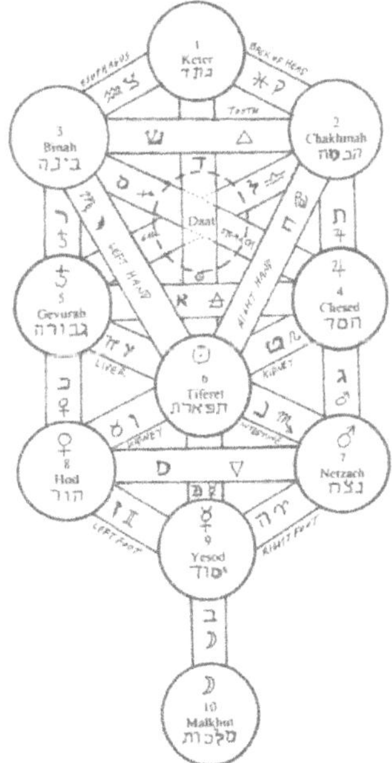

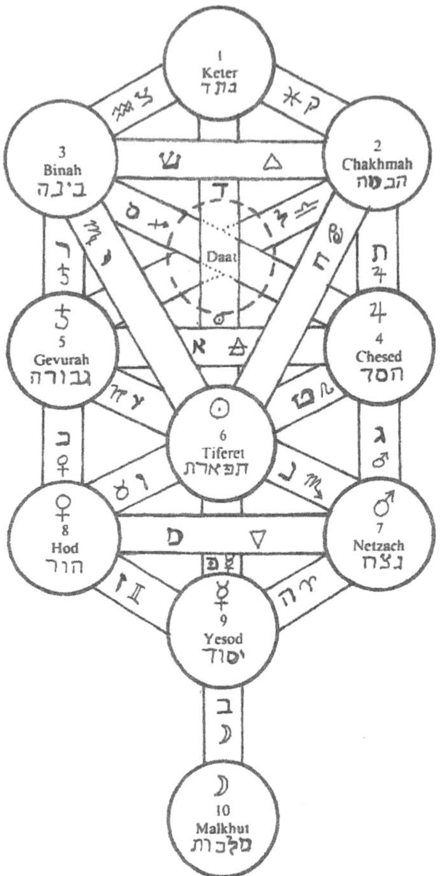

Above is my final diagram of every Hebrew letter on a path, which mirrors both the human body and the Astrological connections. When laid out this way, the above and the below are united, and it also follows in line with the stages of initiation. Furthermore, look at what happens when we look at the bottom two diagonal paths and the vertical path connecting Yesod to Tipereth. If the left foot is placed on the middle path and the right foot is placed on the right diagonal bath we have the step familiar to an Entered Apprentice and we are lopsided to the right of the tree with only the left foot strong on the middle path. Likewise if we place the right foot on the middle path and the left foot on the left diagonal path, we have the step of a Fellow Craft and only the right foot is strong in the middle. However when we place the left foot on the left diagonal path and the right foot on the right diagonal path, then we stand as a Master Mason with both feet aligned with the outside pillars and our body aligned with the middle pillar. We can see the Entered Apprentice standing at Yesod, the Fellow Craft standing at Tiferet, and the Master Mason standing in Daat-each preparing to enter their respective degree.

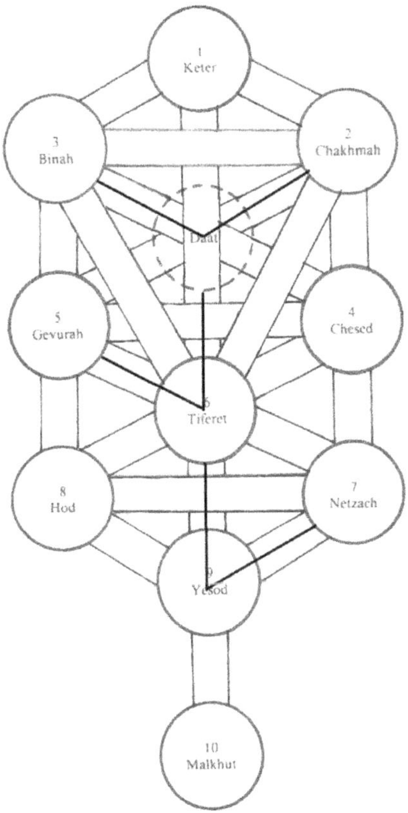

I would also like to make a brief mention of the tarot since many authors have tried to associate the 22 major arcana with the 22 Hebrew letters. In my opinion, Papus (Dr. Gerard Encause)'s association is the most correct, as he demonstrates quite convincingly to my satisfaction that in the earlier decks of tarot, every tarot image actually looks like a particular Hebrew letter. (For more on his associations, one should read his book *The Tarot of the Bohemians*). Therefore the image on the tarot card itself became a memory device for the Hebrew letter associated with it- since the image looked like the Hebrew letter. For example, the Hebrew letter Shin looks like the jester cap of the fool on the Fool card. Or, for example, the Hebrew letter Ayin looks like a tower that is being split in two- which is the image of the Tower card traditionally associated with it. Many schools have suggested that the original association between the Hebrew letter and card was a blind, and that there are in fact other more correct associations- usually in an attempt to force their own connections between the qabbalistic paths. However, based on the simple layout of the qabbalistic tree outlined above, it would suggest that the original associations of the letters are in fact correct.

For example, if Shin is the Fool, then this would place him at the area of the head on the tree- which is in fact where the jesters cap that looks like a shin rests. In the card, he is also about to walk off a cliff and fall down, which is in fact what would happen to someone who blindly walked off this uppermost horizontal path on the qabbalistic tree. Likewise the Magician card would be associated with Aleph, and would be pointing to the above and the below as he sits in the middle of the qabbalistic tree- just like he does on the image of the Tarot card. Or the Hanged Man- associated with Lamed, actually hangs in DAATh, the area between the upper and lower worlds, and in this capacity, he is the next step from the Fool, who fell off the cliff. On page 56 is a diagram of where the Major Arcana cards would be placed according to this system outlined. Meditation on it will reveal that these are very natural places for these cards to be without any forced interpretation. To give a few more examples, the Emperor now resides in the vertical path connecting Tipereth (Beauty) and Kether (Crown)....so he has finally regained his crown! The card of Judgment is now between the Sephirot of Binah (Understanding) and Geburah (actually associated with Judgment)! Finally the cards of the Sun and the Moon both issue from the Crown (Kether). So the three cards and paths connected with Kether become the Sun, the Moon, and the Emperor. Again, Freemasons may see a connection with the Sun, Moon, and Master of the Lodge. So many things come to light with this layout which seems very self explanatory, and they all connect on many levels. This would again imply that this order was possibly intentionally designed this way from the beginning, and many of the keys to it are to be found in Masonic ritual. Over the centuries, well intentioned students of qabbalah have endeavored to explain other possible orders and connections, but again, many of these interpretations just come across as forced. If we accept that they misunderstood the order of where the Hebrew letters should be placed on the paths of the Qabbalistic Tree to begin with, it makes sense why they then began to misinterpret which Hebrew letter was associated with which card- seeing blinds where there were not any.

THE JUGGLER

THE JUGGLER

Above: The Juggler (Magician) looks like the letter Aleph.

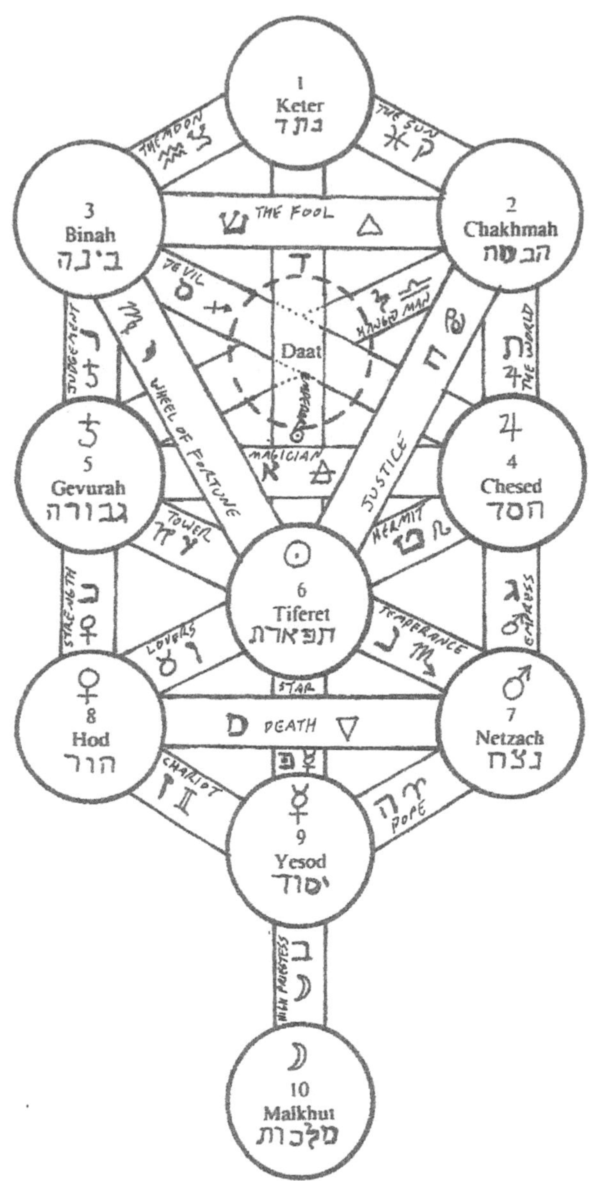

Above: The Qabbalistic Tree with Tarot cards placed on each path.

Above: The Hanged Man card looks like the Hebrew letter Lamed.

I want to stress that even though this order seems to make the most sense, based on all considerations of associations involved and based on the earliest texts on the subject matter, I also recognize that this is certainly not the order that most esoteric schools out there today present the tree. To my knowledge, this particular layout has never before been published, and I take it as a great revelation. The early qabbalists and alchemist were said to be partially concerned with making a Golem, or Homunculus, which was a being in the form of a person that was created out of the elements and qabbalistic letters. As the *Sephir Yetzirah* says in 2:6: "A sign for this thing: Twenty two objects *in a single body*." Based on the associations in the *Sephir Yetzirah*, if we actually lay everything out and place the organs where they would go on a person (basing the tree off of a human body), then this is the pattern that emerges. This particular layout clearly demonstrates many associations of a qabbalistic, astrological, and alchemical nature, and fits the rites of initiation in the ancient mystery schools, and as such, I fully and whole heartedly believe that this may have been the originally intended layout of the qabbalistic tree. It also reveals a pattern that brings new light to the Tarot. Knowing that this layout corresponds to both the human body and the layout of Solomon's Temple in Freemasonry, is it any wonder that we are informed in ritual that we have become *living stones*? Isn't a golem likewise a living stone- according to myth? There are many more mysteries associated with this layout, which reveal many more profound ideas and sciences to those who take the time to meditate on it further. I know it can be a valuable aid to anyone studying this spiritual science and many others associated with it, and it validates and confirms multiple passages found in the *Sephir Yetzirah*, the *Sephir Bahir*, and the *Zohar*. I leave it to qabbalistic students of the future to write more on it.

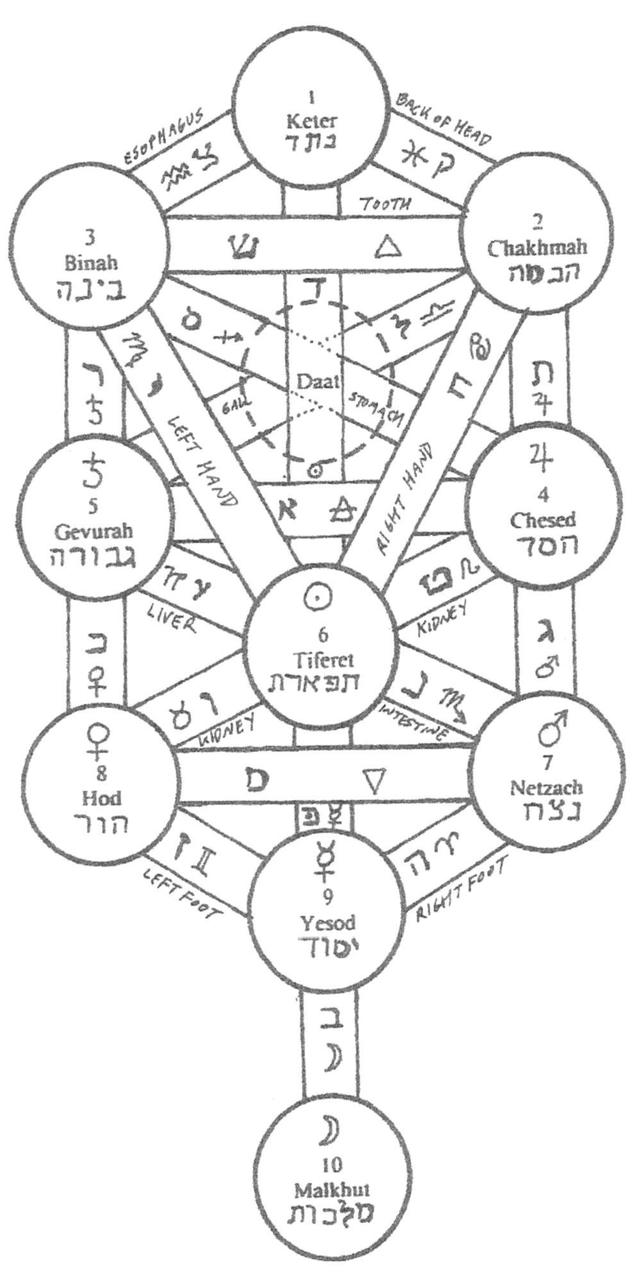
1
Keter
כתר
2
Chakhmah
חכמה
3
Binah
בינה
ESOPHAGUS
BACK OF HEAD
TOOTH
Daat
GALL
STOMACH
LEFT HAND
RIGHT HAND
5
Gevurah
גבורה
4
Chesed
חסד
LIVER
KIDNEY
6
Tiferet
תפארת
KIDNEY
INTESTINE
8
Hod
הוד
7
Netzach
נצח
LEFT FOOT
RIGHT FOOT
9
Yesod
יסוד
10
Malkhut
מלכות

From a Masonic Perspective, we can certainly see in this layout the steps, the pillars, the stages of initiation, the connection between Solomon's Temple and the human body, and other details like the lesser lights and Master Mason's grip. We also see how the 10 sephirot in addition to the 22 letters forms 32 combinations- which is the number of degrees in the Ancient and Accepted Scottish Rite. (For those who doubt a connection between the degrees in the Scottish Rite and the Qabbalah, I will give one connection for researchers to build off of: the 24th degree gives a description of the Hermit card of the Tarot at the beginning, which is associated with Semekh…therefore this degree corresponds to this letter).

We can also see how the sephirot of Malkuth, associated with the moon and salt, comes in contact with the sphere of Yesod which is associated with Mercury, which in turn connects with Tipereth that was ruled by the Sun and associated with Sulphur, and these three alchemical ingredients form the middle pillar. In alchemy these three ingredients formed the Philosopher's Stone (in their proper state). As a side note, they were also associated with the wages of a Fellow Craft with salt=corn, wine=mercury, and sulphur=oil in alchemical texts and diagrams, and they went together to form a stone just like the three components go together to form a corner stone in Masonic ritual. When viewing the qabbalistic tree as an initiation map, the Fellow Craft would possess the corn, wine, and oil of Malkuth, Yesod, and Tifereth, but he would not yet be in possession of the secrets of a Master Mason which only exist in the realm past Daath. If we just look at the middle pillar and the three horizontal bars, this image likewise forms a cross of Loraine- which is a familiar symbol used in the various Rites of Freemasonry. When the two outside pillars are also emphasized, we have the symbol of Jacob's Ladder- another important symbol in Freemasonry.

Some have attempted to further link the layout of the furniture and officers of the Masonic Lodge with the layout of the Sephirot themselves on the Qabbalistic Tree. For example, according to this model most subscribers to this theory place the Worshipful Master at Kether (the Crown) and the altar at Tipereth. The long path between the two where Daath would reside is where the Sanctum Sanctorum, or Holy of Holies would be- in which only the Master can walk (like the Emperor card). While not entirely ruling this theory out, I do think that this interpretation includes many details which often come across as forced, so I am not at this time whole-heartedly willing to accept it as a model. Though if such an interpretation and association proves of value to brothers, and if it empowers them, then I am not going to say it has no merit! I encourage any brother to publish their ideas on the subject and prove me wrong!

Finally, it should be pointed out that one of the main names for God in Hebrew is spelled Yod-He-Vau-He, which has been Latinized to Jehovah. Hebrew is normally written from left to right, but if we spell this name going from top to bottom, the name of God actually forms the image of a person and it looks like the qabbalistic tree itself. What is more, the name of Jesus in Hebrew is spelled Yod-He-Shin-Vau-He, and pronounced Yeheshua. If we do the same thing with it, then the fire of Shin defines the heart in the chest, and becomes the flaming heart of Jesus since it represents fire. We are made in God's image.

Above: (Left) YHVH in Hebrew, (Right) YHShVH in Hebrew.

There are many more ideas associated with qabbalah however, most particularly the subject of gematria- which is alluded to in the second degree of Freemasonry and is found throughout Masonic ritual. Therefore the next chapter of this book will cover this exciting connection. This is the first time that a list of Masonic related words from ritual has been published in relation to the numeric values associated with them. As will be shown, the implications are that it is possible that certain aspects of ritual were carefully chosen in order to emphasize the symbolic values associated with them.

Chapter 3: A Connection With Gematria

One of the sciences in Qabbalah is known as Gematria. Gematria is the substitution of one word for another based on numeric value, with the idea that in the ancient world, (in which letters were also numbers), certain numbers had symbolic value. Therefore since the letters of the Hebrew and Greek alphabets were each designated a number, we can calculate the value of any given word. Within Qabbalah, this science is mentioned in the *Sephir Yetzirah*, which outlines the number value for each Hebrew letter, however we also find this number code associated with Greek letters- which likewise traditionally had a number value associated with them. In fact, the word "gematria" likely comes from the Greek: Γεωμετρια, as it can be related to geometry. In gematria, letters are replaced by numbers, and by extension a word or a phrase can be added up to get a summed number, and by extension certain numbers have a symbolic meaning and/or geometric value. Therefore certain words with the same summed number were deemed to have the same symbolic meaning behind them. It is debated by historians if gematria was first developed by the Hebrews or the Greeks, but it is clear that both used the science regularly.

I feel gematria is alluded to in the second degree lecture of Freemasonry where it says: *"Arithmetic teaches the powers and properties of numbers, which are variously effected by letters, tables, figures, and instruments."* It is also taught in the 27th degree of the Ancient and Accepted Scottish Rite of the Southern Jurisdiction, in the Knight of the Sun or Prince Adept degree (which is the 28th degree in *Morals and Dogma*).

I believe that when several phrases and words in Freemasonry are converted into Hebrew or Greek and then added up, that they have significant symbolic relationships. I do not believe, as some teach, that numbers have "magical properties", or that numbers rule the destiny of a thing. Rather, like the ancient Greeks and Hebrews, I believe that numbers can convey a symbolic meaning which may not be as apparent on the surface. Among the Greeks and Hebrews, they did not use separate symbols all the time for numbers, but rather used their alphabet. Since the Bible is written primarily in Greek and Hebrew, there are symbolic number patterns in my mind, which also show up and are reinforced in the degrees of Freemasonry- either by design or by accident (I'll leave it to you to decide!) Due to the frequency of these significant number patterns in Masonic ritual, I personally have to believe that it may have been by design. I would also like to emphasize that the system of Freemasonry was largely developed in its current form by brothers who would likely have been learned in both Greek and Hebrew, and it would not be unreasonable to assume that they utilized both while compiling aspects of the ritual.

Please refer to the following gematria table on the next page for both Hebrew and Greek.

	1	2	3	4	5	6	7	8
1	Aleph	ࠀ	א	1	Α α	*	Alpha	A
2	Beth	ࠁ	ב	2	Β β	*	Beta	B
3	Gimel	ࠂ	ג	3	Γ γ	*	Gamma	G
4	Daleth	ࠃ	ד	4	Δ δ	*	Delta	D
5	He	ࠄ	ה	5	Ε ε	*	Epsilon	E /H
6	Vau	ࠅ	ו	6	F	*	Digamma	Fv /V
7	Zain	ࠆ	ז	7	Ζ ζ		Zeta	
8	Heth	ࠇ	ח	8	Η η		Eta	
9	Teth	ࠈ	ט	9	Θ ϑ θ		Theta	
10	Jod	ࠉ	י	10	Ι ι	*	Iota	I /Y
11	Caph	ࠊ	כ	20	Κ κ	*	Kappa	C /K
12	Lamed	ࠋ	ל	30	Λ λ	*	Lambda	L
13	Mem	ࠌ	מ	40	Μ μ	*	Mu	M
14	Nun	ࠍ	נ	50	Ν ν	*	Nu	N
15	Samech	ࠎ	ס	60	Ξ ξ		Xi	
16	Oin	ࠏ	ע	70	Ο ο	*	Omicron	O
17	Pe	ࠐ	פ	80	Π π	*	Pi	P
18	Tzadi	ࠑ	צ	90	ϛ		Episemon bau επισημον βαυ·	
19	Koph	ࠒ	ק	100				
				100	Ρ ρ	*	Rho	R
20	Resh	ࠓ	ר	200				
				200	Σ σ	*	Sigma	S /Sh
21	Shin	ࠔ	ש	300				
				300	Τ τ	*	Tau	T
22	Tau	ࠕ	ת	400				
				400	Υ υ	*	Upsilon	U
	Caph FINAL		ך	500	Φ φ		Phi	
	Mem FINAL		ם	600	Χ χ		Chi	
	Nun FINAL		ן	700	Ψ ψ		Psi	
	Pe FINAL		ף	800	Ω ω		Omega	
	Tzadi FINAL		ץ	900	ϡ		Sanpi	

Column 1: Names of the Hebrew Letters; 2: Samaritan letters; 3: Hebrew and Chaldean letters; 4: Numerical equivalents of the letters; 5: Greek letters; 6: Letters marked with asterisks are those brought to Greece from Phoenicia; 7: Names of Greek letters; 8: Nearest English equivalents.

I will also use the following table that shows the English letter associated with each Hebrew letter, since this is unable to be printed in a Hebrew font:

כ	י	ט	ח	ז	ו	ה	ד	ג	ב	א
K	Y	T	Ch	Z	V	H	D	G	B	A
ת	ש	ר	ק	צ	פ	ע	ס	נ	מ	ל
Tv	Sh	R	Q	Tz	P	O	S	N	M	L

Here are phrases, words, and ideas that are frequently found in Freemasonry and their gematria number value. I have put words together with the same numeric value so that it can be seen that they are alluding to possibly the same ideas. Words with a relatively close number value were also deemed to be related symbolically. Also, keep in mind that in gematria "0s" are considered place holders. Therefore the number 888 has the same symbolic value as 8880, or 888000, etc.

"Most Excellent": υπερτερος : 1260
"Solomon": Σολομων: 1260
"Transmute": αλασσω:1262
"Gnosis"(knowledge):ΓΝΩΣΙΣ :1263
"Sun light": ηλεκτωρ :1263

"Cornerstone:Υωνια :864
"Holy of Holies":Αυιων and also in the Hebrew- (Q+D+Sh+H+Q+D+Sh+Y+M) :864
"God": Θεων :864
"Pythagoras":Πυθαγορας :864
"Jerusalem":Ιερουσαλημ : 864
"The word of the Lord from Jerusalem": In Hebrew- V+D+B+R+Y+H+V+H+M+Y+R+V+Sh+L+M: 864

"The stone which the builders rejected":
λιθον ον απεδοκιμασαν οι οικοδομουντες: 2160
"Strong": In Hebrew- G+B+V+R+H: 216
"Lion": In Hebrew- A+R+Y+H: 216
(Think of these in relation to the "strong grip" of a Master Mason, also associated with the lion. Half of 216 has a value of 108, which is another important number as will be demonstrated).

"The Stone which the builders rejected is become the head of the corner":
λιθουου απεδο κιυασαν οι οικοδομουτες ουτος εγενηθη εις κ εφαλην γωνιας: 5180
"Sun": ηλιου :518

"Cornerstone": In Hebrew- P+N+T: 530
"Sun": In Hebrew- Ch+M+H: 530
"Headstone": In Hebrew- A+B+N: 53

"Square": πλαισιον: 451
"Good deed": πραξις:451

"Shibboleth": σιβωλιθος:1307 (date of Templar persecution)

“Sun + Moon”: Ηλιος + Σεληνη: 619
“to raise up”: ανιστημι :619
“True”-or “straight”: ιθυς :619
“sign”: τοσημα :619

“Assembly”: αλια :42
“Together”: αμα :42
“Law”: δικη:42
(Add this number 42 to :To take an oath”: διομνυμι :624), and you get 666 (which has nothing to do with the devil!) In the ancient number canons it just represented physical action as it reached towards the spiritual, which is why Solomon received 666 talents of gold yearly in exchange for bread (1 Kings 10:14), or why Adonikam had 666 children (Ezra 2:3). Other instances of 666 include:
“Let there be light”: In Hebrew- Y+H+Y+M+A+R+T: 666
“Transmission”: παραδοσις :666
“The heart, the soul, the mind”: ηφπην: 666
“Jehova God that created the Heavens”: In Hebrew- H+A+L+Y+H+V+H+B+V+R+A+H+Sh+M+Y+M: 666
“The head of the corner”: In Hebrew- L+R+A+Sh+P+N+H” 666
“Sarapis” (who was Osiris-Apis): οΣεραπις: 666
“I am God on earth”: Θεος ειμι επι γαιης : 666
“From God”-παρα θεου-666
Many Christian traditions end prayers "in the name of Jesus", or "in Jesus' name". In Hebrew, Jesus is spelled yod-he-shin-vau-he and has the following number correspondences: 10+5+300+6+5= 326. "Name" or “shem” in Hebrew is spelled shin-mem and has the following number correspondences: 300+40= 340. Therefore if we add Jesus+name= 666. This is a good example of how prayer "in Jesus' name" represents action via gematria, and how it follows in line with the ancient symbolic number codes. Obviously this clearly shows that if 666 is found in "Jesus' name" then it cannot also be associated with the devil. Incidentally- it should be

observed how “Jesus” in Hebrew is spelled the same as the Hebrew name for G-d (yod-he-vau-he), only the Hebrew letter “shin” is inserted in it.

“An ark, in which a few, that is eight souls were saved through water” (I Peter 3:20):
κιβωτον εις ην ολιγοι τοντ εστιν οκτωψυχαι γιεσωθησαν δι υ δατος :8880
“I am Jehovah, I change not” (Malachi 3:6): In Hebrew-
A+N+Y+Y+H+V+H+L+A+Sh+N+Y+T+Y: 888
“Jesus”: Ιησους :888
“The Seven Churches” (from Revelations):
Η Επτα Ηκκδηιασ: 888
“Salvation of our God”: In Hebrew-
Y+Sh+V+O+T+A+L+H+Y+N+V: 888
If we add “Ether” (ΑΙΘΗΡ)= 128 to Heaven (ΕΜΠΥΡΕΙΟΝ)= 760, we get a sum of 888.

(Let us not forget that our 24 inch gauge in Freemasonry is divided into three sections of eight each- or 8:8:8).

“In the beginning God (as Elohim)”: In Hebrew- B+R+A+Sh+Y+T +A+L+H+Y+M: 999

“Enoch”: In Hebrew H+N+Khaf Final: 555
“Foundation”: ιδρυμα: 555
(Also of significance is the fact that the Washington Monument is 555 feet high- as a giant hollow pillar, like what Enoch erected according to legend).

“Threefold”: τρισσος :1080
“Holy Spirit”: το πνευμα Αγιον:1080
“Jesus+Mary”: Ιησους + Μαπιαμ :1080
“The earth spirit”: το γαιον πνευμα:1080

“fountain of wisdom”: πηγη σοφιας :1080
“The Lord is in his Holy Temple, let all the earth keep silent before him” (Habakkuk 2:20): In Hebrew-
Y+H+V+H+B+H+Y+K+L+Q+D+Sh+V+H+M+M+P+N+Y+V+K +L+H+A+R+Tz: 1080
“God himself that formed the earth and made it”: In Hebrew-
H+V+A+H+A+L+H+Y+M+Y+Tz+R+H+A+R+O+V+O+Sh+H: 1080

“Pillar”: οτυλος :1200
“Cord”, “rope” or “cable”: οχοινος :1200
“Light”: λυχνον:1200

“Horus”: Ωρος :1500
“Light”: φως :1500
“Secret”: τυφλος :1500
“Eye”: ωψ:1500

“Altar”: θνσιαστηριον:1358
“Perfect Knowledge”: επιγνωσις :1358
“Of the sun”: Ελιωτις :1358
“Word”: φωνη :1358
“The Great Gnosis”: η Μεγαλη Γνωσις :1358
“Knowledge and Truth”: Γνθσις και Αληθεια:1358

“Behold I lay in Zion a chief cornerstone” (I Peter 2:6):
ιδου πθημιεν Σιων λιθον ακρογωνιαιον :3330
“Lord of Lords”: κυριος των κυριων :3330

“Hiram Abiff”: In Hebrew- H+V+R+M+A+B+Y+V: 273
“The Stone Which the Builders Rejected”: In Hebrew-
A+B+N+M+A+Samech+V+H+B+V+N+Y+M: 273

(Incidentally, in Hebrew, this phrase is pronounced "Eben Masu Ha-Bonim". Look closely: "Eben (Ma)su (Ha)-(Bon)im.

Let me give a Hebrew gematria word that is significant in Freemasonry. The word for "east" in Hebrew: QDM (Qudem), has a value of 144, which is 12 x 12. The number 144 shows up frequently in the Bible as a significant number in itself. So maybe there is an association here? After all, we are ordered to "look to the East" in Masonic openings. In alchemy the word for "regulus" in Hebrew: DN MLK, also adds to 144- and it implied "Mastery" or "Kingship". So "Mastery" and the "East" are both connected in Hebrew.
To take this a step further, the following words also add up to 144:

"Eden" in Hebrew-K+O+D+N: 144
"Lebanon" in Hebrew- V+L+B+N+V+N: 144
"Qabal"- or "to receive" in Hebrew (related to qabbalah)-
V+Q+B++L+V: 144
"Forehead" in Hebrew- M+Tz+Ch+V: 144
"Blow" in Hebrew- N+P+V+Ch: 144
"Deliver" in Hebrew- Ch+L+V+Tz: 144
"Lazarus": λαζαρε: 144

So "to deliver" "a blow" to the "forehead"- all add up to 144, which is the same value as "to receive", "Eden", "Lebanon", "East", "Mastery", and "Lazarus" (in Greek). They all appear to be related in Masonic ritual. After the blow to the forehead is delivered, each brother is raised like Lazarus. (In *The Alchemical Keys to Masonic Ritual* this connection is covered thoroughly).

At least in the ancient world, numbers symbolized ideas. So some numbers had geometric value, other could associate with time, and others, when broken down, could illustrate a philosophical concept. Let me give a few different examples. In Greek, the God

Abraxas, the god Mithras, the Nile, and the god Belenos all were associated with the cycle of the sun throughout the year, and thus by extension were also associated with time. All four individually add up to 365 in Greek, thus associated with the number of days in a year. The Gnostic symbol of Abraxas can also be found on old Templar seals, thus suggesting that at least some of the leadership of the Knights Templar were prone to understanding and perpetuating secret knowldge.

Mithras-ΜΕΙΘΡΑΣ-365
Abraxas-ΑΒΡΑΣΑΞ-365
River Nile-ΝΕΙΛΟΣ-365
Belenos-Βεληνος -365

Numbers may also convey a geometric value.

So for another example, in the Bible we are taught that Jesus miraculously caught exactly 153 fishes. (What we are not told is that according to the earlier Pythagorean writings, Pythagoras is also said to have miraculously caught 153 fishes). It just so happens that the symbol we know as the "Jesus fish" today, which is found on automobiles all across the United States, is formed by intersecting two circles that are equal in diameter, so that the edge of each crosses the mid-point of the other. When this happens, we can create a cross within the fish symbol (called a Vesica Pisces) formed by the two circles which is formed by the mid-point diameter of the two circles crossing the vertical center line of the "fish". The ratio of the long axis to the short axis is 265/153. In the early writings of the Pythagoreans and other Greeks, they abbreviated this measurement by calling it "the measurement of the fish" or sometimes just by the number "153". This is why, I believe, Jesus and Pythagoras were said to have caught 153 fishes, as it was a geometric metaphor. This "measurement of the fish" is what is used to make a perfect equilateral triangle. Interestingly, "the Magdalena" in Greek (η Μαγδαληνη), adds up to 153, and "Mary" (Μαρια) adds up to 152. (See diagram on next page).

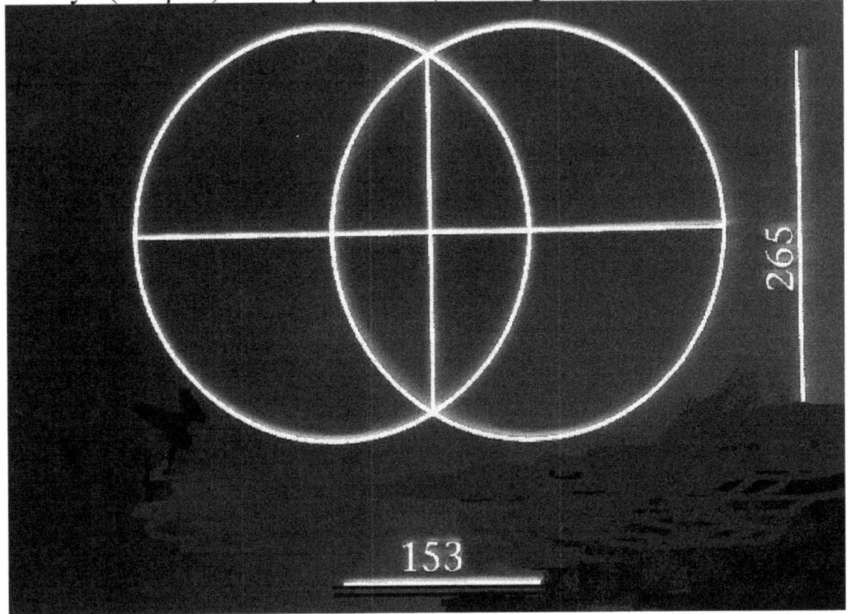

Let me give another example: In Greek, Hermes= Ηρμης= 353 (when every Greek letter is converted into its numeric counter-part and the whole word is added up). Zeus= Ζευς= 612; and Apollo= Απολλων=1061. Geometrically, if we were to create three circles next to each other, each with a diameter measurement of 353.666, thus each corresponding to the number of Hermes. Then draw a larger circle around those three smaller circles, and the diameter of the bigger circle will be 1061, the number of Apollo. Then if we enclosed two medium circles within the bigger circle that end up forming a Vesica Pisces, and which completely enclose all three of the smaller circles so that everything is connected to everything else, the long arm of the mid-point of the Vesica Pisces will have a value of 612- the number of Zeus.

We can also see the use of the vesica pisces in relation to Hebrew when we consider the relation between God, Adam, and Eve. If we assign the vertical long axis the value of Adam (ADM)= 45, and we assign the short axis the value of God (YHVH)=26, it forms the correct ratio proportion. Since Adam was made in God's image, we can relate this composite symbol to representing all of Adam. However we are told that Eve was made by taking a rib from Adam- which is in fact what part of the vesica looks like. If we subtract the name of God (YHVH)=26, from Adam (ADM)=45, then we end up with the number 19. This just happens to be the number that Eve (ChVH) adds up to in gematria. It should also be pointed out that some of the other words that add up to 26 are the words "love" and "unity"- or ABHA and AChD. Also, as mentioned previously, if we take the sephirot of the middle pillar and add them together 1+6+9+10=26.

The Pythagoreans took it a step further and may add up all the final numbers in something to reduce it. Thus 365 became 3+6+5= 14, and then 1+4= 5. So the root value is 5. The Pythagoreans associated several qualities to numbers 1-10. Here are a few:

1= the Monad and Unity (God-source).
2= The Dyad and duality, opposites- Heaven and Earth.
3= The Triad, harmonium, reconciliation, third reaction point from interaction of dualities.
4=The Tetrad, matter, nature, stability.
5= The Pentad, man incarnated, quintessence, lack of strife, light.
6= The Hexad, union of material and spiritual, mystical marriage, Gnosis (divine knowledge).
7=The Heptad, completed cycle, universal power, due measure, completion.
8=The Octad, steadfastness, harmony on an earthy or cosmic level.
9=The Ennead, assimilation, all opposite forces return to source, earthly perfection, perfection of the cosmos.

10= The Decad, eternity, God in manifestation, All, divine omnipresence, return to unity.

These same concepts later got reinforced within the qabbalistic tree, which has ten emanations or sephirot. Similar attributes of the Pythagoreans have been ascribed to each of the sephirot.

Finally, there was another Pythagorean method that was used in the past, and that was to add up the sum of all the numbers within a number. So, for example, the number four, sacred to the Pythagoreans and what they took their oaths on, was a symbol of material world, and is composed of 1+2+3+4= 10. Therefore 4 (or the material world) has the complete potential of the eternity of God in manifestation. The Pythagoreans depicted this with one dot, then two dots, then three dots, then four dots in the form of a triangle which was called the tetraktys, and the connecting of the dots within the figure formed many interesting shapes of manifestation which also had symbolic value. It is interesting to speculate that with some modern superstring theories, they depict the Universe in a model of 10 dimensions, which collapse into our 4 dimensions of space-time, much like what Pythagoras was alluding to with his theory. Along these same lines, it is also interesting to note that just as all the letters of the Hebrew alphabet come from the letter "Yod", this letter has a numeric value of 10.

The Pythagoreans also had a "greater tetraktys" which was composed of 27 points forming a triangle, which is also an important symbol in the 32nd degree of the Scottish Rite. If we apply the same model of adding 1+2+3+4+5+6+7……all the way to 27, then the sum total is 666- again relating as a number of uniting the spiritual and the material in action. The Pythagoreans also assigned geometric shapes for each number they were attempting to depict symbolically. For example, "6" could be depicted as a six pointed star or a hexagram- familiar to

Freemasons as Solomon's Seal. This seal furthermore has 60 degrees between all of its angles.

Gematria allows us to examine Greek and Hebrew texts in a new light, and with new meaning- including passages in the Bible that are also emphasized in Freemasonry. That being said, these numbers are also found in the architecture of temples around the world, and in ancient measurements. For example, the Roman half-pace of 1.216512 ft divides exactly 108,000,000 times into the earth's mean circumference, and 1080 square megalithic yards are equal to 888 square yards in English measure.

There were also philosophical ideas expressed by a number repeating, like 777, 888, 999, or even 555. In this instance, the number being repeated was being emphasized. For example, there is a reason why Jesus adds up to 888, or Enoch sums to 555 (or why the Washington monument is exactly 555 feet high!) There were also opposite forces depicted. For example, in the ancient number canons, 666 was associated with action on both the physical and spiritual planes, whereas 1080 was associated with inner receptivity and inward attunement. So they were like Yin and Yang. Though both add up to 9 through the Pythagorean method, and both harmonize to the same source. If we add 1080 and 666, we get 1746- which may be considered a number of balance. Some of the phrases that add up to 1746 in Greek from the New Testament include:
Grain of mustard seed-κοκκος σλναπεως– 1746
The Glory to the God of Israel-η δοξα του θεου Ισραηλ– 1746
The Universal Spirit- το πνευμα κοσμου– 1746
The Hidden Spirit-το κεκκρυμενον πνευμα–1746
The Treasure of Jesus-ο θησαυρος Ιησου– 1746
The Divinity of Spirit- η θεοτης πνευματος– 1746
Precious Pearl of Mary- τιμιος μαργαριτης Μαριας– 1746
Gnosis (knowledge) of God-γνωσις θεου– 1747

The Chalice of Jesus- το ποτηριον Ιησου– 1746
Jerusalem, the city of God- Ιερουσαλημ, η πολις θεου– 1746
The City of the Saints of God-η πολις αγιων θεον– 1746

This puts a completely different meaning behind the parable of "the Kingdom of Heaven is a grain of mustard seed", as it suggests that Heaven is attainable through balanced living- much like our three degrees emphasize in Freemasonry. It also provides insight to "Gnosis of God" and the "Chalice of Jesus"- both associated with the Holy Grail.

Sometimes by adding one word with symbolic meaning to another, it will produce a new number of symbolic meaning- like when we add "to take an oath" with "assembly", and it equals 666- the same value as "let there be light", and also "from God" in Greek adds up to 666. So it is reinforced three times in Freemasonry at the same time in the first degree, which suggests to me that it is more than coincidence. (I'm sure that this may just be fuel for uneducated anti-Masons who do not understand number theory).

The word for "corn" or "wheat" in Greek is: σιτος and it has a numeric value of 780.
The word for "wisdom" in Greek is: Σοφια and it also has a numeric value of 780.
Wisdom- or *Sophia*, was likewise traditionally associated with a goddess, and as such, she was likewise associated with Virgo, the Virgin, which is also associated with wheat or corn. In fact early talismans and sculptures of the goddess Sophia and of Virgo regularly depict the figures with wheat or corn. Virgo was also associated with distillation in alchemy- which some see alluded to in the second degree of Freemasonry both by the penalty of the obligation and the corn hanging over the water for the second degree password. Interestingly, when viewed from the air, the French cathedrals of Chartres, Etampes, Notre Dame du Paris,

Reims, Leon, Amiens, Rouen, Bayeux, and Evereux form the constellation of Virgo on the ground. Many authors have pointed to the fact that it was the Knights Templar that provided the initial funding and creation and funding of these cathedrals, and it will also be recalled that they were suppressed in 1307. The Greek word of Shiboleth has a numeric value of 1307. For those who have read *The Secret Architecture of Our Nation's Capital: The Masons and the Building of Washington DC*, by David Ovason, it will likewise be recalled that the cornerstones of the monuments of Washington DC were likewise laid by Freemasons when Virgo was prominent in the Heavens.

Moses and his burning bush are featured in the York Rite. There are a couple theories on how Moses' name in Hebrew should be spelled, with one theory being that it is spelled Mem-Shem-Aleph (MShA)- the three "mother letters" in qabbalah. However another spelling of "Moses" in Hebrew is with the three letters Mem-Shin-Heh (MShH) which has a Gematria of 345. On the other hand, the Hebrew name by which G-d first announces Himself to Moses in relation to the burning bush is Eheyeh Asher Eheyeh which has the following Gematria values:

Eheyeh (AHYH)= (21)
+ Asher (AShR) (501)
+ Eheyeh (AHYH) (21)
= Total of 543 .

Thus Moses (with a Gematria value of 345) is an exact reflection of G-d (with a Gematria of 543). In other words, we see opposite sequences in 543:345. In this we may also see the idea of the first creation, in which the "spirit of God hovered above the water and said let there be light..." Some have pointed out that Moses' name means "drawn from the water", and of course, when you hover over water you see your own reflection. So in a sense, a new creation is symbolically taking place in this context. It is interesting that fire and water are thus united between the burning bush and Moses. This same number of 345 may also be directly interpreted as “God Almighty” (El Shaddai) with AL ShDY (1+30+300+4+10). It is also found in “The Name”- H ShM (5+300+40)= 345. In Freemasonry we also see 345 emphasized in relation to Pythagoras and the discovery of the 47th Problem of Euclid, in which a triangle is composed of the rations of 3:4:5 on its sides. This ratio of 3:4:5 was likewise used by the alchemists for the proportions of 3 parts sulphur (oils), to 4 parts salts, to 5 parts mercury (alcohol), and so the triangle can often be found featured in old alchemical diagrams. Likewise, some have seen the burning bush itself in relation to Moses as an alchemical metaphor, which in this case may define proportions based on the gematria value attached to it. Also interesting, if we add this name of God to Moses’ name, we get 543+345= 888.

We should also look at the story of Boaz and Ruth since both are found in Masonic ritual. Boaz is spelled Beth(B)-Ayin(O)-Zain(Z) in Hebrew, which have the following numeric associations: B:2, O:70, Z:7. Therefore added up "Boaz"=79. Ruth is spelled Resh(R)- Vau (U)- Tav (Th) in Hebrew, which have the following numeric associations: R:200, U:6, Th:400. Therefore added up "Ruth"= 606 in Hebrew. Now, since Boaz and Ruth get together to produce a child (Ruth 4:13), and since Ruth started out as a servant working in the field (and thus harvesting), one could say that it is a story pointing to producing fruitful ends (both in the field and in reproduction). Well, it just turns out that the Hebrew word for "fruitful"- spelled Tav, Pe, Resh, He, has the numeric values of Tv:400, P:80, R:200, H: 5= 685. This number, 685, is what you get when you add Boaz+Ruth. Therefore Boaz+Ruth= Fruitful.

Finally, what happens if “Jachin” and “Boaz” are put together? After all, they were the names of the two pillars on the outer porch of Solomon’s Temple, and as such, they would also relate to the outside pillars on the qabbalistic tree diagram. We have already demonstrated that the word “Boaz” in Hebrew adds up to 79. “Jachin” on the other hand is spelled Y+K+Y+N in Hebrew, and can equal 90 or 740 (depending on whether we add the Nun as a regular Nun with a value of 50, or a Nun Final with the value of 700).Therefore Jachin+Boaz will have a sum of either 169 or 819. The following are other words in both Greek and Hebrew that add up to either 169 or 819:

“Happiness” in Hebrew- M+O+D+N+H: 169
“The Amen”: Ο Αμηv: 169
“Stone”: λιθον: 169
“Simple Oneness” in Hebrew- A+Ch+D+V+Th+ P+Sh+V+T+H: 819
“Son of he who is like God (Michael)”: B+N+S+Th+V+R+M+Y+K+A+L: 819
“To sanctify” in Hebrew: H+Q+D+Sh+Th+Y: 819
“To know”: Ειδω: 819

So these are just a few examples of the many gematria correspondences out there, in which association has been found within Freemasonry. I personally like the fact that “to raise up” (and thus make you a Master) and Sun+Moon have the same number value- as the lesser lights are the Sun, Moon, and Master of the Lodge. I felt it important to put a few of these ideas out there so that brothers can examine it themselves. To my knowledge, even though the idea has been suggested through many authors, I have never seen a complete list like this that relates specifically to Freemasonry, so I thought it best to finally provide one. There are other gematria correspondences in the symbolic Lodge degrees that are outlined in the ritual lecture of the 27th degree in the Ancient and Accepted Scottish Rite (SJ). For those interested in this subject, they would be wise to go back and listen carefully to the lectures in this Knight of the Sun or Prince Adept degree. It should be stressed that the qabbalistic science of gematria extends well beyond passages from the Bible that are found in Freemasonry, but it is significant in my mind that the majority of the passages found emphasized within Freemasonry have gematria correspondences. Also, I will emphasize that most of these numbers patterns, and certain others, are predominate symbolic numbers in many ancient traditions world-wide, and are also reinforced in the architecture of ancient temples. For example, you will see 108, or 1080, or 10800, show up all over the place, and all over the ancient world. One example is according to Hebrew tradition, the hour is divided into 1080 sections, because it was believed that a person takes 1080 breaths in an hour. There are also 1,080 bricks on an Indian fire altar, 108 flowers on an Indian wedding wreath, 10,800 stanzas in the Rig Veda, 108 moves in Tai Chi- just to give a few of the many examples. Many of these ideas are further developed in my book *Revelation of the Holy Grail*, written under my esoteric name of Chevalier Emerys.

So gematria may have much to teach us in the form of symbolic number. Qabbalists have spent a great deal of time combing through the Pentateuch in an effort to find the number codes within it. Christian qabbalists have endeavored to use the same science in examining the New Testament in both Greek and Hebrew. The Qabbalistic texts like the *Sephir Yetzirah*, the *Sephir Bahir,* and the *Zohar* all emphasize the number/letter relationship, and we find the same idea emphasized in Freemasonry. By exploring this science, not only can number patterns begin to emerge from sacred texts, but these same ideas lead to geometric form and the emphasis of philosophical ideas. We know that compilers of both the old and new Testaments were concerned with teaching mathematical relationships and incorporating philosophical ideas. For example, in I Kings vii. 23, and 2 Chron. Iv.2) we read: "Also, he made a molten sea of ten cubits from brim to brim, round in compass, and five cubits the height thereof; and a line of thirty cubits did compass it round about." In this passage the molten sea is round and measures 30 cubits round about (in circumference) and 10 cubits from brim to brim in diameter. Thus we are given a value of 30/10=3…which seems to be pointing the right direction towards the value of pi in the more accurate 3.1415. This was obviously intentional in order to convey a lesson for those who studied it. Much of the Bible is this way, and it just so happens that many of the passages that emphasize certain number patterns are also the passages and words that are emphasized in the degrees of Freemasonry. This suggests that possibly compilers of the degrees had these thoughts in mind while compiling them. If nothing else, seeing these connections in the degrees can provide further meaning and the speculating on them may open up other possibilities. One could spend a lifetime attempting to convert all of the passwords, words of recognition, and scriptural quotes that are in the degrees into Hebrew and/or Greek and then converting them to their numeric code. I have presented this section on gematria as a starter for those who wish to explore it further.

Chapter 4: What Does It All Mean?!

I have covered a lot of qabbalistic information that may relate to Freemasonry in a relatively short space. The study of qabbalah can last a life time, and as these symbolic relationships are being learned and studied, one is usually prone to ask themselves, "Why am I spending my time doing this? How is this adding to the quality of my life?!" Or they may find themselves saying, "I have learned all these codes and symbolic meanings, but I'm still left wondering why such an elaborate code needed to be created to perpetuate truth?!" Qabbalah was designed to awaken and challenge all aspects of one's being- physical, mental, and spiritual. Therefore each requires its proper exercise in order to function to its fullest capacity. This model can be found to a certain degree within the three main degrees of Freemasonry itself- with the EA degree giving us physical challenges, the FC degree giving us mental challenges, and the MM degree giving us spiritual challenges. Ultimately however, everything in qabbalah is just a sign post- pointing in a direction. It is for us to follow and to seek attunement. Once we learn the map, we can venture out into the territory. It would be a mistake to think the map is the territory however. Another way of looking at it, is that the qabbalah is a mirror that we can hold before ourselves and before the world, in order to see a meaningful reflection.

Different qabbalistic scholars and different schools have chosen to interpret qabbalah in slightly different ways. There is a fundamental model uniting all however, and we can certainly find the shadows of this model within Freemasonry itself. This suggests that as Freemasonry developed into its current form, these ideas associated with qabbalah were incorporated into it, if they were not there from the beginning. Coming to understand these associations between qabbalah and Freemasonry then opens up the Masonic student to further light. New patterns start to emerge, and new connections form within the consciousness of each Freemason. It has been suggested that as Entered Apprentices, each brother is a bearer of burden with grunt tasks. Fellowcrafts on the other hand begin to understand the order behind the work they are doing, though they are still concerned with labor. Master Masons however, see all of the order behind the work. The compasses lay out the invisible arcs that define the geometry of the shape and mass. If this is the case, then the Master Mason is also concerned with the building plan, or layout of the temple itself. Qabbalah provides this building plan, as it provides the hidden direction and order behind the design. Therefore as Master Masons it falls upon us to at least understand some of what qabbalah has to offer.

Some Masonic brothers have interpreted the role and forms of the apron itself as having qabbalistic significance. For example, the apron by itself is considered a symbol for Yesod by some authors. This is because it covers the genitals and represents mastering the energy of Malkut and putting it to work by beginning higher pursuits with Yesod. The apron of an Entered Apprentice then, has represented a general layout of the tree ahead that needs to be traversed. It is like a map, with the three points of Keter, Chochma, and Binah being the flap, and the square below it being the remaining body of the qabbalistic tree. The apron of a Fellow Craft then represents the journey partially up that tree, where part of it has been explored. The apron of a Master Mason then signifies the brother who stands at the path of Shin- the area of the Sanctum Sanctorum, in which we see a downward flap formed by the paths of Shin, Yod, and Cheth. The rest of the Tree then below it then forms the body of the apron from which the brother had come from and Mastered. See dark outlined images below for the Master Mason apron association on the tree.

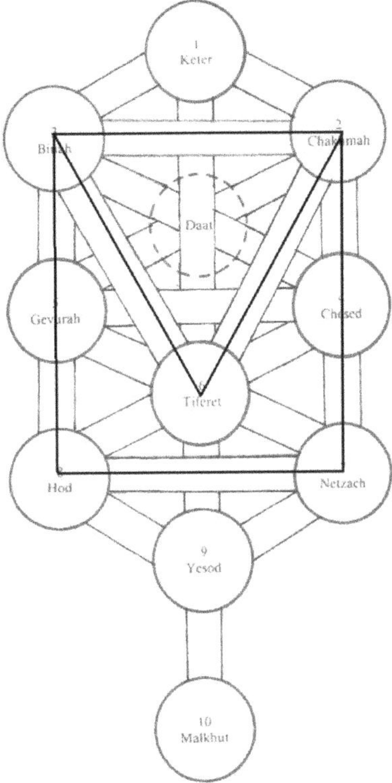

Some have seen qabbalah incorporated by Freemasons beyond just the temple ritual, as it can be found in the actual layout and design of buildings themselves. For example, many Lodge buildings are constructed with storage and general day to day functions at the bowels or basement of the building, the dining area at the stomach of the building, the lodge room at the area of the chest with the heart and throat of the building, and finally the library on the upper level- or head of the building.

We can also project the Qabbalistic tree on to a cathedral like Notre Dame, and see Malkuth as the area outside the cathedral, Yesod at the entrance, with the Baptismal font at the Mem level of water. We see the area of Tiferet where the general congregation resides, and the choir at the area of Daath and the Aleph path of air. The Sacrament is then kept at Kether, and all functions of the presiding officiate take place at Binah and Chochmah and the path of Shin. Since the cathedrals of Notre Dame were modeled off of King Solomon's Temple, this should not be surprising. In applying the same idea to the layout of a Masonic Lodge, we are informed in American work that a blazing star exists on the floor-below the altar. An examination of the Qabbalistic Tree will in fact show that a five pointed star is formed by the paths associated with Binah, Chochma, Chesed, Geburah, and Tiferet.

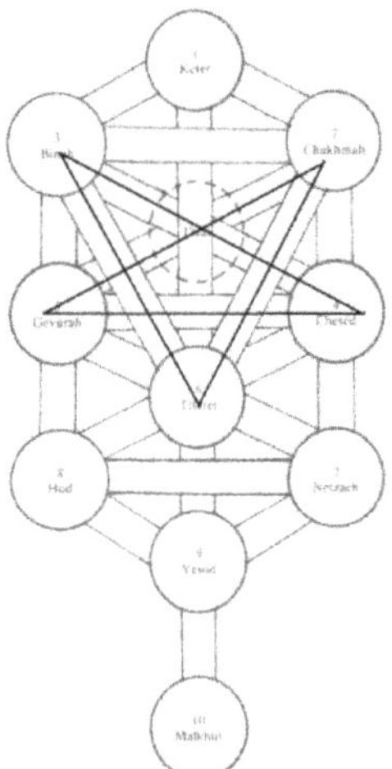

However this symbolism can be found extended even further. We certainly can see the influence of the qabbalistic tree on the layout of the governmental structure of the United States. The Government of the United States is composed of three pillars: Executive, Legislative, and Judicial, and it is composed of four levels- Individual, State, Federal, and A Nation Under God. We see this exact same layout in the qabbalistic tree, with its three pillars and four levels. Therefore the United States government actually stands as a layout of Solomon's Temple- no doubt partially due to the Masonic influence in its founding.

Other authors have seen qabbalah show up in Freemasonry in particular with such things as the "cabal tow", which Pike and other authors saw potentially linked with "qabbalah tow"- or that which "receives" us into the qabbalistic tradition. Qabbalah has certainly also been quick to use word play and association as a means of conveying truth. Other more fanciful theories have suggested that the very word "calvary"- from where we get "chivalry", as related to the old French, is alluding to "qabbalahry"- as "c" and "q" are interchangeable and "v" and "b" are interchangeable from language to language translation. Therefore a French Knight- a *chevalier*, becomes a "qebalae"- or "qabbalah". While not wholeheartedly accepting this idea as a legitimate historical connection of the past, it is not out of the realm of possibility that it was considered within Freemasonry, which is prone to emphasizing such knighthood in certain Rites and bodies.

The qabbalistic tree has likewise been called by different names that are related to Masonic ritual. To give an example, one name for it was "Jacob's Ladder", as it is like a ladder that descends from heaven, and which has three principle rungs on it (which we showed related to Shin, Aleph, and Mem, and by extension the penalties of the three degrees of Freemasonry). The ladder rests in Malkuth- the Kingdom, which has been symbolized by a cubic stone. This is the foundation stone that everything rests on. This is why if someone hasn't prepared this foundation stone by mastering the general physical elements of their life, and thereby becoming free, that they are not ready for the next step into initiation.

The steps of initiation going from water to air, and air to fire in Freemasonry can even be found in the name of the main character in the drama- Hiram Abif. “Hiram” in Hebrew is ChRM. Fire, in Hebrew, is called ChAMAH, air in Hebrew is called RUACh, and water in Hebrew is MAYIM. The first letter of each of these words is Ch-R-M…which spells: “Hiram”. Therefore the very name of Hiram can be pointing us in the direction of the stages of initiation we need to go.

Other qabbalistic scholars have seen the four sephirot on the middle pillar of the Qabbalistic Tree, and the three vertical steps between them, as representing the seven psychic centers, or “chakra”, of the human body. These represented areas of consciousness development that were tied to the genitals (Malkut), the stomach (Yesod), the solar plexus (the path of Mem), the heart (Tiferet), the throat (the path of Aleph), the brow (the path of Shin), and the Crown atop of the head (Keter). The area of Daat was deemed a hidden eighth area at the nape of the neck- the area where the ganglia exists that connects the nerves that go both to the pineal gland of the brow, the eyes, and the radial nerve that goes to the thumb and two forefingers. In fact, Saints are depicted holding these fingers up for this reason in old murals. The seven centers were also associated with the seven seals of Revelations. However other qabbalistic schools teach that the seven psychic centers are associated with the seven lower sephirot, which in turn where associated with the seven planets, and by extension, the seven liberal arts and sciences. It should also be mentioned that the seven areas have likewise been associated with the three rungs on Jacob’s ladder in addition to the four cardinal virtues discussed in Masonic ritual.

Some have used the qabbalistic tree as a meditation mandala, whereas others have used it as a ritual magic guide, and yet others have used it as an early periodic table of elements for alchemical processes. It has applied to the body of the human being and to architecture. It has applied to levels of the human consciousness and levels of material reality. It is found in the Bible, and it is connected with Tarot. The qabbalistic tree truly is a blue print for all of creation, and the qabbalistic sciences have revealed symbolic truths in the form of words. We can see the wisdom of John when he said, "In the beginning was the word, and the word was with God, and the word was God". It is the words of creation that define creation itself. Such qabbalistic ideas can likewise reveal a numeric code for a new understanding of scripture.

This all implies that there is a rich tradition, which when learned, can open up new perceptions of the world and means of creation. Understanding the context of qabbalah and how its symbol sets manifest in the human consciousness can reveal a new language of reading the thoughts behind creation itself. In other words, by understanding these symbol sets, as found in nature, we come to a greater understanding of the blueprint and thoughts of God in creation. In the past, the disciplines of sacred geometry, Hermeticism, alchemy, and Gnosticism have been linked with Qabbalah, as different expressions of the same universal truths. Of course, there are elements of all of these disciplines within the degrees of Freemasonry and other schools of the western esoteric tradition. Coming to understand one of the above mentioned disciplines naturally helps to ease one into an understanding of all the others. The ideas behind these disciplines have been the building blocks of civilization itself.

I should also mention that there are other sciences within Qabbalah that are beyond the scope of this book. However I will mention them as they may provide value to the student who wants to pursue them further and find connections within ritual. These are the processes of *Temurah* and *Notarikon*. Temurah involves the anagrammatizing of words, whilst the Notarikon allows words to be constructed from the initial letters of other words, or sentences can be produced if the component letters of one word were used as the initial letters of others. For example, in Freemasonry, a "sword of light", may become a "sol"- utilizing the first letter of each. "Sol" is the Latin word for "sun". Or, for another example, "Gomar", "Oz" and "Debar", the Hebrew words for wisdom, strength, and beauty, become GOD. The same idea is found in the example of how Chamah, Ruach, and Mayim go together to form ChRM, or Hiram.

Everything outlined in this book should clearly demonstrate to us that Qabbalah is a fundamental backbone of Masonic ritual. If any Craftsman is to understand the passwords, signs, due guards, and other aspect of ritual, then they must at least have a general understanding of Qabbalah. As the fourth degree of the Ancient and Accepted Scottish Rite (SJ) tells us, "Qabbalah is the key to Masonry". By understanding the fundamental qabbalistic associations within Masonic ritual, and seeing how these connect with other esoteric disciplines within Freemasonry like alchemy, new spiritual sciences open up that allow one to see the world in a new light, and thus become Masters of their creation in life. Hopefully this book will act as a beginning study of the subject so that each degree witnessed will open up new perceptions and thereby provide the further light each aspirant seeks.

How and Why?

Now that we have seen some correlations between the qabbalah and Freemasonry, we need to ask ourselves how did this make it into Masonic ritual, and why was it put in there? There are various theories behind when sacred sciences started to make their way into Masonic ritual, with some scholars thinking that these ideas can be found in it from the beginning, and some scholars thinking they were relatively later additions in the 18th century. Others researchers, like myself, take a middle ground and feel that the seeds of the sacred sciences were in Freemasonry from the beginning, but they were not expounded on in the ritual itself until the 18th century.

We know, for example, that many of the Masonic symbols and even the outline of the penalties on the body showed up in earlier alchemical texts as old as Albert Magnus' 1650 work of the *Philophia Naturalis*, and earlier in the works of Robert Fludd in 1619, and Michael Maier's works of 1618. We find other aspects of Masonic ritual in alchemical plates going back as far as 1526, in Aquinas' *De Alchemia*, and the image of the Master Mason's apron shows up in the cipher symbols of Valentinus in 1659. Even people like Isaac Newton studied the symbolism behind Solomon's Temple in his effort to understand alchemy, and some have suggested that the tree he discovered gravity under was actually the Tree of Knowledge of the qabbalah, and it was all a metaphor. These early alchemists were also qabbalists, and the qabbalah was a fundamental part of everything they wrote on.

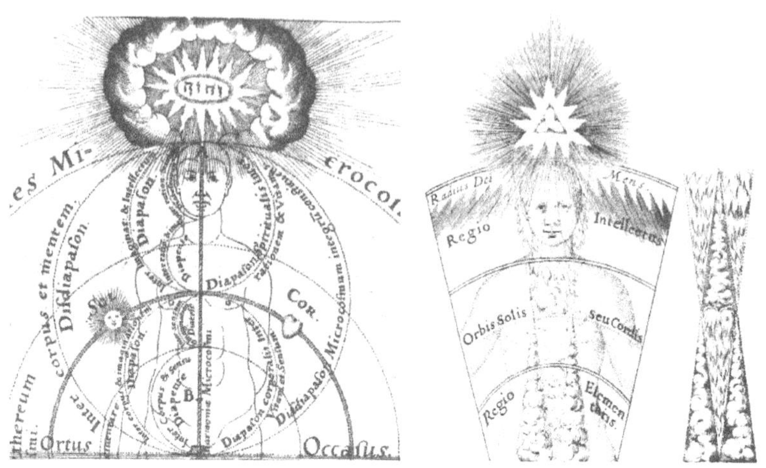

Above: Two plates of Fludd's *Diapason closing full man*, showing divisions, from 1621.

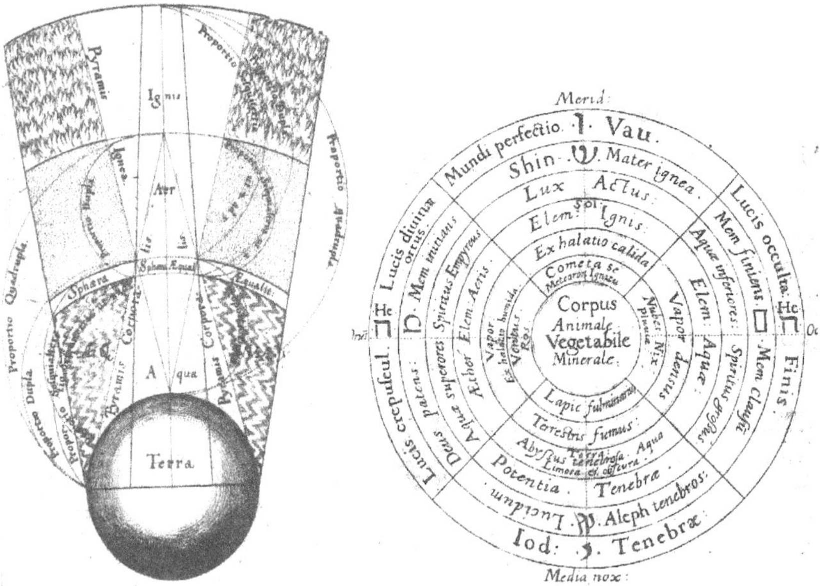

Above: Fludd showing similar progression with the elements in his works of 1620.

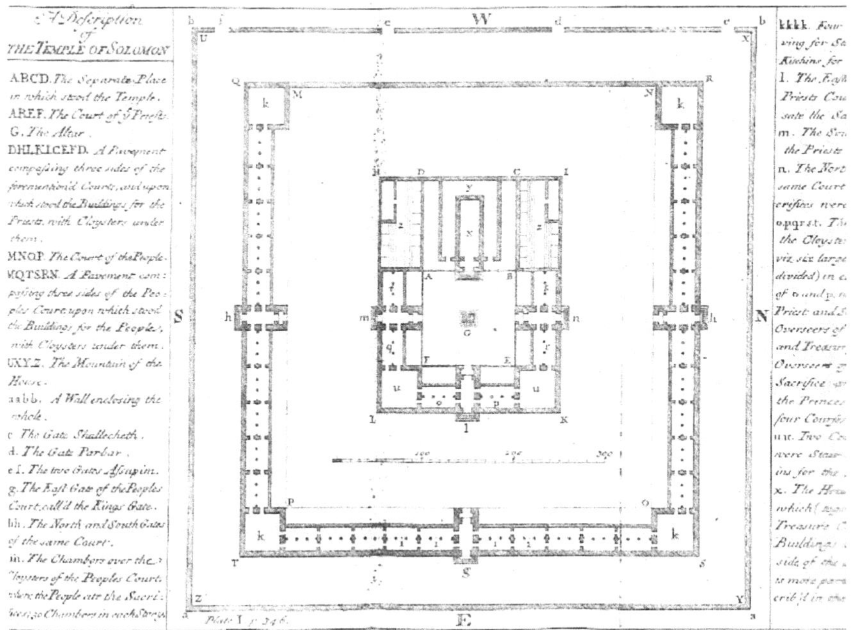

Above: Newton's diagram of Solomon's Temple.

However we can also trace this same alchemical tradition as far back as the cathedral builders of Notre Dame and Chartres, and by extension the Knights Templar who helped finance their production. Since Solomon's Temple is a fundamental aspect of qabbalah, alchemy, and the cathedrals themselves, then we need to ask why the Knights Templar were involved in the creation of these books in stone, and why this got inserted into Masonic ritual.

I will not go into the theories behind how Freemasonry could have come out of the Knights Templar (their full title being the Poor Knights of Christ of the Temple of Solomon), as it has been exhaustively explored by other authors elsewhere, and I cover it in *Revelation of the Holy Grail*. What I will say however, is that while the Knights Templar were in the Holy Land, they were exposed to a number of different esoteric sciences and disciplines which they had not encountered before, and by the time they lost their effort in defending the Holy Land, it is very likely they were making plans on how to build a New Jerusalem in Europe. It also goes without saying that they were likely questioning if material structures were really worth fighting for in an effort to gain a closer connection with God. Since they had been exposed to qabbalistic, alchemical, Hermetic, and Gnostic thought, it also seemed a logical extension to begin to apply these ideas as metaphors to internal processes and development. Therefore the true Solomon's Temple was formed anywhere they met to worship God...*as it was something found within*. By the time the Knights Templar were suppressed, the cathedral age of construction ended, and the symbolism and ideas had to be taken underground. It is here that we likely find the connection with Freemasonry.

Above: Two carvings of many at Notre Dame cathedral in Paris which outline qabbalistic and alchemical processes. The one on the left has Jacob's ladder with ten levels- like the Qabbalistic Tree. The one on the right shows one of the last stages in which a Templar holds a lion shield extending its paw. It was associated with one of the last stages of fire calcinations and the completion of the "Red Lion" in alchemy. In Freemasonry it relates to the Master Mason degree.

What started out as vague references to symbolism associated with Solomon's Temple in the 1600s of Masonic history, later developed into a flourishing of more developed ritual- based on the mouth to ear meaning behind the symbolism being embellished in the 1700s and 1800s. With more Masonic research being done as to the origins of the tradition, more aspects were then added to the rituals themselves in order to further support the hidden meanings behind it all. This brings us to the Masonic ritual as it stands today, which is now largely perpetuated without many members having any idea what it all means! It could be argued that it is coincidence that all of these qabbalistic ideas are found within our modern Masonic rituals, but I do not believe this is the case. Albert Pike recognized the meaning and symbolism by the time he wrote his *Morals and Dogma* and *Esoterika*, and since his time there has just been more and more research done to champion the idea. If it is all coincidence, then we have to be left feeling that there is still a divine plan unfolding unconsciously by those who have perpetuated the tradition, as there are just too many elements found to be ignored.

As Albert Pike says in *Morals and Dogma* (pg 754):
"It is said in many places in the Sohar, that all things that emanate or are created have their root above. Hence also the Ten Sephiroth have their root above, in the world of the garment, with the very Substance of Him… These circles are ten in number. Originated by points, they expand in circular shape."

And on page 777:
"He who desires to attain to the understanding of the Grand Word and the possession of the Great Secret, ought carefully to read the Hermetic philosophers, and will undoubtedly attain initiation, as others have done; but he must take, for the key of their allegories, the single dogma of Hermes, contained in his table of Emerald, and follow, to class his acquisition of knowledge and direct the

operation, the order indicated in the Kabalistic alphabet of the Tarot."

Ultimately, both Qabbalah and Freemasonry are meant to be tools in aiding people in self discovery, consciousness development, and moral responsibility. Each seeks to express the divine through symbolism, and the symbolism in both is largely the same. Therefore one is a reflection of the other, and both are means towards understanding our relationship with God, and God's relationship with creation. Meditation on this science can only bring greater levels of Mastery, and by extension they reveal the mysterious science and patterns behind the other disciplines of Hermeticism, alchemy, and Gnosticism. Hermeticism was the root tradition, Qabbalah was the esoteric science of the Hebrews, Gnosticism was the esoteric doctrine in Christianity, and alchemy was the secret science held by custodians in Islam. The Knights Templar united all of these doctrines while in the Holy Land, and gave birth to the Masonic system as we know it today. Or at least, such is the legend perpetuated by Pike in the Knight Kodosh 30th degree of the Ancient and Accepted Scottish Rite (SJ).

Masonic historians will argue forever about the validity of these legends within the Masonic system, but the important thing is to ask ourselves if they have relevance to ourselves and our world today? I believe they do, and as such, their study adds that much more richness to our experiences in the fraternity, as it gives us meaning behind our actions. Actions without meaning are hollow, but action with meaning implies intention- which is the first step in Mastery. I hope this book has provided meaning and that has furthered the idea that Freemasonry does indeed hold profound qabbalistic secrets. I also hope that these few words on the subject will inspire others to seek out and study the subject more, as this book only scratches the surface. There is so much more that can be said of the subject in Freemasonry, but I will leave it for others…

Selected Bibliography

Barry, Kieren, *The Greek Qabalah: Alphabetic Mysticism and Numerology in the Ancient World*, Samuel Weiser, Maine, 1999.

Chevalier Emerys, *Revelation of the Holy Grail*, 978-0-6151-5878-5, Lulu Press, 2007.

Charpentier, *Louis, The Mysteries of Chartres Cathedral*, translated by Sir Ronald Fraser, RILKO Books, Athenaeum Press, Sussex, 2002.

Churton, Tobiuas, *The Magus of Freemasonry: The Mysterious Life of Elias Ashmole: Scientist, Alchemist, and Founder of the Royal Society*, Inner Traditions, Vermont, 2004.

Dan, Joseph, *Jewish Mysticism and Jewish Ethics*, Jason Aaronson, NJ, 1996.

Fulcanelli, *Le Mystere des Cathedrales*, translated by Mary Sworder, Brotherhood of Life Inc, 2000.

Godwin, Joscelyn, *Robert Fludd: Hermetic Philosopher and surveyor of two worlds*, Phanes Press, Grand Rapids, MI, 1979.

Guthrie, Kenneth, *The Pythagorean Sourcebook and Library*, Phanes Press, Michigan, 1988.

Hall, Manly Palmer, *The Wisdom of the Knowing Ones*, Philosophical Research Society, Los Angeles, 2000.

Hall, Manly Palmer, *The Secret Teachings of All Ages,* Philosophical Research Society, Los Angeles, 1988.

Hall, Manly Palmer, *The Lost Keys of Freemasonry*, Philosophical Research Society, Los Angeles, 1923.

Hanson, Kenneth, *Kabbalah: Three Thousand Years of Mystic Tradition*, Council Oak Books, San Francisco, 1998.

Hogan, Timothy, *The Alchemical Keys To Masonic Ritual*, 978-1-4357-0440-4, Lulu Press, 2008.

Hoyos, Arturo De, *Scottish Rite Ritual Monitor & Guide*, The Supreme Council, 33*, Southern Jurisdiction, Washington DC, 2007.

Kaplan, Aryeh, *Sefer Yetzirah: The Book of Creation*, Weiser books, San Francisco, 1997.

Kaplan, Aryeh, *The Bahir,*, Weiser books, San Francisco, 1997.

Knight, Gareth, *A Practical Guide to Qabalistic Symbolism*, Samuel Weiser, Maine, 1991.

MacNulty, W. Kirk, *The Way of the Craftsman*, Central Regalia Limited, London, 2002.

MacNulty, W. Kirk, *Freemasonry: A Journey Through Ritual and Symbol, Thames and Hudson*, New York, 1991.

Macoy, Robert, General *History, Cyclopedia and Dictionary of Freemasonry*, Masonic Publishing Company, New York, 1870.

Mackey, Albert Gallatin, *The History of Freemasonry*, Masonic History Company, New York, 1898.

Michell, John, *The Dimensions of Paradise: The Proportions and Symbolic Numbers of Ancient Cosmology*, Harper and Row, San Francisco, 1971.

Ovason, David, *The Secret Architecture of our Nation's Capital: The Masons and the Building of Washington D.C.,* Harper Collins, London, 1999.

Papus, The Tarot of the Bohemians, Melvin Powers, Hollywood.

Papus, *The Qabalah: Secret Tradition of the West*, Samuel Weiser, Maine, 2000.

Pike, Albert, *Morals and Dogma*, The Supreme Council of Southern Jurisdiction, Charleston, 1953.

Pike, Albert, *Esoterika: Symbolism of the Blue Degrees of Freemasonry*, Scottish Rite Research Society, Washington DC, 2005.

Roob, Alexander, *Alchemy & Mysticism*, Taschen, New York, 1997.

Saint Martin, Louis Claude de, *Tableau naturel des Rapports qui existent entre Dieu, L'Homme et l'Univers*, 2 vols, 8vo, Edinburgh, 1782.

Scholem, Gershom, *Kabbalah*, Keter Publishing, Jerusalem, 1974.

Scholem, Gershom, *Origins of Kabbalah*, Princeton University, 1990.

Sperling, Harry and Maurice Simon (translators), *The Zohar, volumes 1-5*, Soncino Press, London, 1984.

Stone, M, *Jewish Writings of the Second Temple Period*, Van Gorcum and Co, 1984.

Townley, Kevin, *The Cube of Space: Container of Creation*, Archive Press, Boulder-CO, 1993.

Wolfson, Elliot, *Along the Path: Studies in Kabbalistic Myth, Symbolism, and Hermeneutics*, State University of New York Press, New York, 1995.

White, Michael, *Isaac Newton, The Last Sorcerer*, Fourth Estate Limited, Great Britain, 1997.

Z'ev ben Shimon Halevi, *Adam and the Kabbalistic Tree*, Samuel Weiser, Maine, 1974.

If you enjoyed this book, other books by **Timothy Hogan** include:

The Alchemical Keys to Masonic Ritual:
This is the first book to explore in depth how the passwords, penal signs, due guards, and emblems of the symbolic degrees relate directly to the alchemical process for producing the Philosopher's Stone. This book is intended for Masons who wish to gain further light into the secret meanings of their tradition. The Keys given for the first time in this book may be one of the most important working tools ever given to the Master Mason wishing to understand his craft.

ISBN: 978-1-4357-0440-4

Revelation of the Holy Grail (by Chevalier Emerys):
The Holy Grail has become a popular field of study in recent years, however most books on the subject are written by authors who are not themselves initiated into the mystery school tradition of the Grail. Revelation of the Holy Grail is one of the first books on the subject which is written by an initiate within several of the Knighthood Orders associated with the Grail Tradition. This book provides many previously unpublished facts about the history and tradition of the Grail movement, which includes some of the most influential people in human history. The Quest of the Holy Grail has proved to really be about the quest for human civilization. It has spawned not only the greatest political movements in history, but also it has been the cornerstone of human technology. Alchemy, Hebrew Mysteries, Templar Secrets, ancient technologies, Gnostic traditions, and secret societies have all been involved in this exciting history which is the backbone of our modern day world.

ISBN: 978-0-615-15878-5

Entering the
Chain of Union

Timothy Hogan

Entering the Chain of Union

Entering the Chain of Union explores different esoteric, spiritual, and initiatic traditions from around the world and illustrates how they share similar doctrines and rituals. This book is a firsthand account by a western initiate as he examines traditions as diverse as Gnosticism, Hermeticism, Sufi, Druze, Taoist and Tibetan alchemical doctrines, Egyptian mysteries, Mayan traditions, and an exploration of many sacred monuments from around the world. It is also a firsthand account of his meeting with spiritual leaders of different traditions, including Harun Yahya. This book will be particularly interesting to anyone with a background in Templarism, Freemasonry, Rosicrucianism, or Martinism. This book follows some of Timothy Hogan's travels as he attempts to do The Great Work.

ISBN: 978-1-105-57105-3

***Novo Clavis Esoterika*:**

Brazen Serpent Press
Novo Clavis Esoterika - a deluxe, hand-bound in leather limited edition of 555 signed and numbered copies. *Novo Clavis Esoterika* contains copiously illustrated and expanded versions of Timothy Hogan's critically acclaimed *The Alchemical Keys to Masonic Ritual* and *The 32 Secret Paths of Solomon*, as well several key texts on Martinism, Gnosticism, alchemy, and the Hermetic Tradition.

About Timothy Hogan:

Among some of his accomplishments, Timothy Hogan is the Grand Master for the Ordre Soverain du Temple Initiatique (OSTI) Knight Templar lineage, and runs its outer organization of CIRCES International. He is a Past Master of East Denver #160 Masonic Lodge (AF&AM) and active member of Enlightenment Masonic Lodge #198 (AF&AM). He is a former District Lecturer for the Grand Lodge of Colorado (AF&AM). He is a Knight Templar in the York Rite and a 32° Knight Commander of the Court of Honor (KCCH) in the Ancient and Accepted Scottish Rite of Freemasonry (SJ). He has been knighted into the Royal Order of Scotland as a Rosicrucian Knight of Kilwinning and in the Knight Masons of Ireland as a Sir Knight of the East and the West. He is a Past Sovereign Master of Allied Masonic Degree Chapter 425. He is an active officer in the Societas Rosicruciana In Civitibus Foederatis Colorado College. He is a Past Master of the Rocky Mountain Lodge of the Ancient Mystical Order of Rosicrucians (AMORC), having completed 9+ degrees. He is also a Past Master of the Rosicrucian Lodge of the Phoenix and the Grail. He is a Gold-Star Sir Knight of the Knights of the Glen. He has been initiated into the Tibetan Phowa practices of Bon Buddhism by the venerated K.C. Ayang Rinpoche of Tibet. He has also been initiated in various other Orders of Pythagorean, Martinist, Alchemical and Hermetic lineages, and served in leadership capacities within these traditions.

Timothy Hogan regularly lectures around the world at lodges and Grand Lodges on the western mystery tradition and has appeared on numerous televised broadcasts in both the United States and Turkey, as well as numerous pod-cast interviews. He is also a regular contributor to *Living Stones Magazine* and www.thesanctumsanctorum.com, and has published in *Heredom vol. 17* of the Scottish Rite Research Society.

Above: Timothy Hogan on Dateline NBC

www.ingramcontent.com/pod-product-compliance
Ingram Content Group UK Ltd.
Pitfield, Milton Keynes, MK11 3LW, UK
UKHW020239250726
13967UKWH00001B/460

9 780557 046102